LIFE'S WORTH

Life's Worth

Love in an Era of Servitude

Tim Grossi

LIFE'S WORTH

INTRODUCTION

The following historical romance is a fictional story about two people in love and separated by circumstances beyond their control during an era where human servitude took many different forms and was a large part of everyday life. Breaking those bonds and living free, truly free, is a central theme to the story, as well as living a life within those limitations and making the best of any situation.

I ask the reader to be cognizant of the events that transpired and the correlation between these events and the role the different forms of servitude played in their occurrence. It was eye-opening for me and hopefully will be for you as well.

PROLOGUE

Jem Baker straddled the uppermost yard of the foremast. When he was atop the yard and looked out at the open ocean, a sense of calm came across him, and he thought of his beloved Kisis. It had been over three years since he had seen her last. Although her presence was felt in his heart, her memory waned. He could not let that happen. He was half a world away, and he did not know whether he would ever see her again. But he was free, free from his servitude to the British Navy, free to make his way through life as he saw fit and free to keep her memory alive by daydreaming of his homecoming.

There was no daydreaming that day. He had a job to do! The captain had ordered all sails unfurled. He was on the right yardarm, and his best friend Billy was on the left. The ship had three masts: the mainmast in the middle, the mizzenmast to the stern, and the foremast toward the bow. Each sail had an upper crossbar, or yard, that held the sail. When unfurled, a halyard was used to unfurl the sail. Halyards are ropes that use blocks and tackles to let the sails down. The bottom of the sail was attached to a yardarm under the main yardarm to secure the sail.

Jem and the others unfurled the sails and slid down the

foremast to attach the topsails to the yards. As they went ascended to the top yards, they saw e the *Amity* attacking the *Fateh Muhammad*, the second of the large Mughal treasure ships. The outgunned *Amity* was taking the worst of the battle, yet it still fought the bigger ship, causing extensive damage. *The Fancy* came around at full sail to broadside the *Fateh Muhammad's* stern. Jem had a bird's-eye view of the battle from his perch on the foremast yard.

The captain had ordered this top crew to stay put so that as soon as they pulled alongside for a broadside; the sails were to be furled to stop any movement of the *Fancy*. As the *Amity* pulled alongside the *Fateh Muhammad*, the *Fancy* came around and gave the *Fateh Muhammad* a broadside to the stern as the guns bared. Captain Avery then rammed the stern of the *Fateh Muhammad* and ordered sails furled. The ship stopped and swung around like a lever, and with grappling hooks, *the Fancy* pulled alongside backward to the *Fateh Mohammed* on the starboard side, opposite the *Amity* on the port side. The battle ceased when the *Fateh Muhammad* was boarded on two sides by two different crews. Although the Mughal ship had more soldiers and sailors, the pirates were more ruthless, subjugating the crew within minutes.

Once the sails were secured, Jem and Billy almost flew down the rigging and grabbed cutlasses stowed near the bow. They joined the battle, climbing onto the Mughal ship. By the time they arrived on the deck, the fighting was over.

All hands searched the ship for treasure, and Jem witnessed firsthand the brutality of men seeking treasure. They quickly tortured the captain and several officers to find the location of the cargo. Jem could not believe what he was watching. There was such rampaging and crazed brutality.

The slave rowers from below deck, probably forty in all, were brought to the main deck and inspected. Jem was amazed at the different races of the slaves. He guessed there were Chinese or Japanese, Northmen, Europeans of all kinds, Africans, and some islanders. The Mughals enslaved many of the people that came from every walk of life. Jem had experienced slavery firsthand, and he did not like any part of it.

Only ten or twelve of the slaves were considered healthy and were given cutlasses and knives. It wasn't long before they were slashing at their Mughal masters with abandon, killing them, throwing them overboard, and inflicting revenge for the pain and brutality they had suffered at their captor's hands.

Jem looked to the *Amity* and saw Captain Tew lying dead in a pile of his intestines; his abdomen had been eviscerated by a cannonball. He approached Captain Avery on the stern forecastle of the *Fateh Muhammad*, and Jem motioned to the dead Captain Tew lying on the severely damaged *Amity*. Captain Avery took charge of both ships.

They found the treasure hidden in the *Fateh Muhammad*, which was vast, including gold and silver bars, gold coins, spices, textiles made of silk and cotton, stores of grain, and other merchandise. The *Fateh Muhammad* was a prize. Once the *Amity* was repaired to sailing status, both ships would head to Madagascar for further repairs and the sale of the prize ship.

The *Ganj-i-Sawai* (pronounced Gun-Ji-Sa-vie) was the larger ship and had more treasure, so it was to be the next target. Since the *Amity* was severely damaged and without a captain, Captain Avery ordered all the treasure quickly stowed on the *Fancy*, kept only thirty crew and the slaves on the Amity, and took the rest of her crew of one hundred onto the *Fancy*, to chase and capture the *Ganj-i-Sawai*.

ONE

Young Jem skipped rocks over the still waters of the Chowan River. His father, James Baker, tended a fire on the eastern bank of the river, twenty yards from the river's edge, which has a broad, rocky riverbed, ending against a brush apron. He kept a close eye on his six-year-old son, who liked to get into mischief.

In his early thirties, James was medium height and powerfully built, one who was used to manual labor. He had very light brownish blond hair, blue eyes, and a round face cleanly shaven, most of the time. He had built a huge fire pit ringed by large stones. He propped grated sticks over the fire to dry and smoke the fish they had caught. It would take most of the night and into the next day to finish salting and smoking the incredible number of fish that would feed his family for several weeks in the coming winter. The brackish, tidal river teemed with different kinds of fish, mainly large striped bass, which was an excellent and diverse food source.

James prepared to cook some of the fish for their evening meal when he heard Jem racing toward the camp. Just south of where Jem was skipping rocks, James saw two figures walking up the river. The tall man was accompanied by a small girl, who he guessed was the same age as Jem. By the way he bore himself straight and upright, he was undoubtedly from the Chowanoac Tribe.

The Chowanoac was thin, about five feet, nine inches or so in height, and he walked with a regal bearing. He was dressed in the customary Chowanoac dress, with a long skirt or loin cloth that covered both the front and back of his waist. He also wore a dyed deerskin around his chest like a toga, exposing one arm. He wore very nice moccasins. His head was scraped on one side of his head, and on the other side, his black hair was tufted with an attached coxcomb, or a small feather wrap, around the base of the tuft.

The young girl had a type of deerskin top on, which covered her upper torso. She too had a style of loincloth similar to the man's loincloth. Her moccasins were old and scuffed, like any young child's shoes would be. Her raven black hair was long and shaggy with bangs in the front.

Because of the recent war between the tribe, white settlers, and the Tuscarora, there were issues surrounding the outcome and a reluctance to be friendly with all strangers. The man raised a hand in greeting, and James returned the greeting. James motioned for them to come into his camp and eat, rubbing his stomach and moving his fingers and thumb towards his mouth, miming eating.

The Chowanoac hesitated, looked at the little girl who was transfixed on the strangers and decided to accept the offer. They approached the fire and set their packs down. The Chowanoac grasped James's forearm in a friendly greeting; James returned the warmth. The local customary greeting was used to show friendship. James offered for them to sit. He looked at the man and said, pointing to himself, "James."

The guest looked back and said, "Skiko," pointing to himself. He then pointed to the young girl and said, "Kisis" (pronounced *Ki-zee*).

James pointed to his son and said, "Jem."

They all smiled and were glad there were no long names to remember, which usually happened. Jem gawked at Kisis, looking her over from head to foot. Her eyes were dark set and large with black pupils. Her face was thin with high cheekbones, ending with a strong jaw and chin. Jem looked at her and then at her father, questioningly, "Is he her father, Papa?"

James looked at Skiko and motioned to his face and then to Kisis's face, that they looked alike. Skiko motioned back that she was not his daughter but his granddaughter from his son. James was able to make this connection after long minutes of motions, words, signs, and drawing in the dirt. Once he figured it out, they all smiled. James motioned that Jem was his son, which was comprehended immediately.

Skiko looked at the fish and then at the fire. He motioned to James to look at what he had. From his bag, he pulled out two large, orange objects that looked like potatoes. James knew they were sweet potatoes, and had heard of them, but he had never eaten any. Skiko scraped the potatoes with his knife and then thinly sliced them, but not too thin. He rubbed some kind of grease on them and placed them on the stones around the fire to cook. He then motioned to James to sprinkle some salt on them for flavoring, rubbing his stomach in a yummy gesture.

Kisis looked at Jem and motioned to him regarding throwing the rock in the river. Jem looked at his father and asked, "Papa, can we skip stones in the water?"

"Yes, but stay right in front of us, and don't wander off. And… stay out of the water."

Kisis spoke to her grandfather, and he probably gave her the same direction and warning James had given Jem. The two children ran to the water and Jem picked up the first stone. He skipped it across the water about four times and looked at Kisis with a proud smile. Kisis picked up a rock, threw it, and it sank immediately. Jem laughed and turned to see her staring at him with a look of contempt, her jaw clenched and slightly moving side to side. Jem knew he had upset her and would become familiar with that look in the future. He picked up a flat rock, motioned with his hand and wrist how to throw it, and gave it to Kisis. She grabbed it from him, somewhat forcefully, and skipped the stone across the water. She looked at him with a satisfied look, as though *I can do anything you can do.*

Jem grabbed another stone and skipped it about five times across the water. Kisis grabbed a stone and skipped it only twice. Jem laughed out loud. As he bent down to grab another stone, Kisis grabbed a large rock and hurled it into the water at Jem's feet. The splash hit him in the face and Kisis laughed and laughed. Jem laughed too, but grabbed a rock and threw it in the water at Kisis's feet, wetting her.

It was on.

Before the adults could stop the revelry, both kids were wet and laughing hysterically. They almost had to be carried back to the camp. It was a chilly night and their clothes had to be dried. They were both wrapped in blankets and sat next to the fire, giggling about their water battle.

Supper was something they all enjoyed. The fish and the sweet potatoes were both delicious. Jem asked, with a mouthful, "Papa, are these sweet potatoes? They taste good."

James exclaimed, "Yes, they are. We *must* learn how to grow them. They are tasty."

James motioned to Skiko and through their sign language was able to communicate regarding the growth of the sweet potatoes. Skiko motioned he would bring some to James and show him how to plant and raise the vegetable. James motioned in the dirt in the direction of his farm and how long it would take to get there. Skiko in turn, let him know where he lived and the distance from where they were. The men did not live far from each other. It was about a nine-hour walk. Skiko lived in a camp on the river, and James had a farm inland. They were each about four hours from home where they spent the night.

The next morning, their clothes were dry, and they dressed for the day. The two youngsters set about picking berries and nuts for breakfast to eat with the left-over fish from the night before. Skiko showed James an easy way to make a travois out of the wood he had, which would be a much easier way to move the smoked fish, rather than carrying it.

After breakfast, Skiko and Kisis packed their belongings and said farewell. Before they left, James drew a map in the dirt for Skiko to follow to his farm. Skiko knew the land well and motioned with five fingers he would visit in "nanan" (five) suns, pointing to the sun, or five days.

That afternoon, on the way home, Jem did nothing but talk about Kisis and how they had such a good time. James knew his son was smitten but didn't let on. He liked both Skiko and Kisis very much. They were amicable and not much different from him and his family.

When they got home, Jem told his mother all about the encounter and what a good time he had. She looked at James and smiled that mother's smile. She had never heard Jem talk about a male friend the way he talked about Kisis. There was an instant bond she knew was evident.

Two

The Baker homestead sat in a small valley approximately eight miles northwest of the settlement known as the town on Queen Anne's Creek, in later years renamed Edenton. The twenty acres were part of a resettlement plan that took place after the Chowanoac War of 1676-1677.

At one time, the Chowanoac people were the largest tribe of the Algonquin-speaking tribes that inhabited eastern North Carolina and tidal eastern Virginia. Their largest city, which was called Chowanoke, was estimated to have over 2000 inhabitants and 700-800 warriors. Through disease, inter-warring with other tribes, and settler encroachment, they waged war in 1676 against the white settlers, which ended in defeat. Many of their warriors were enslaved, and the remaining inhabitants were relegated to Chowanoke (the first established reservation in North America). These lands they had already inhabited were given to them.

Their remaining lands were then up for resettlement and the then Lord Proprietors of Carolina offered these parcels to settlers in the Albemarle portion of Carolina. The Charles Town portion of Carolina (South Carolina) had just been formed and had not been settled until several years later. Settlers from the Virginia Colony came with their dreams and could purchase the land for less than what other lands were sold for in the Virginia Colony.

James Baker grew up in Boston the son of parents who were indentured servants, who came to America from England in the second wave of English immigrants. Boston was just beginning to grow, and the Bakers were held to their servitude longer than was originally arranged.

Indentured servitude, an institution of bound labor due to debt, was the driving force of settlement in the colonies up until the Revolutionary War. It served as the vehicle to populate the new world with a labor force that was financially unwilling or unable to make the journey across the ocean. A new life with opportunity would hopefully be free after the debt was paid. The population in the mid-17th century and the first half of the 18th century was two-thirds indentured servants to one-third freemen.

Many investors in this institution were businesspeople who sometimes took advantage of the situations and were not upstanding and forthright in their contracts with individuals, given their connections to the nobility. These colonial aristocrats were mirror images of those in England, which people were subject to and tried to escape from. The Puritan settlement of Boston also established religious constraints which were not popular to indentured servants of other religious affiliates. Jonathan Baker, James's father, was a baker by trade. He was an important part of the Boston community. His skills as a baker were highly regarded and much needed. However, he was not a Puritan, and all knew it.

The Puritans came to this new land seeking religious freedom. Once here and established, they became what they left England and Europe to escape, as was evident by the hanging of Mary Dwyer in 1660 because she was a Quaker. Quakers were forbidden in the colony at that time. Jonathan Baker wanted his family to be able to live their lives free from business or religious constraints.

Jonathan looked at his son and said, "James, we came to this country seeking the freedom to live our lives as we wanted. I've always instilled in you to choose a life of freedom to do as you please. Boston is not that place. We are not Puritans. I've saved enough money for you to travel ahead of the rest of the family to Virginia. Land costs less there and they do not have the restrictions Boston has."

James said, "How will I know what to buy?"

Jonathan answered, "My servitude will be up soon. If you cannot decide what to buy or where to buy, live there until you figure it out. We will follow as soon as the debt is paid in full."

James liked Boston and saw how quickly it was growing. He knew many people through his schooling and caught the eye of a young lady who came from an influential family. Her name was Margaret, and she was educated, intelligent, and had an independent streak similar to James's. They fell in love and then came headlong into issues, into life.

Although highly regarded for his talents by the community, Jonathan Baker was an indentured servant and not a Puritan. His son was not up to the social level of Margaret and therefore not regarded as a suitable beau.

Margaret, on the other hand, was educated as a teacher and hated the Puritan constraints of her family and her community. Women were held in low regard, and this infuriated her. When James was given the opportunity to relocate, she accepted his marriage proposal and escaped with him.

The Virginia colony was not dominated by a specific religion and land was said to be available. Once in Jamestown, the capital of Virginia, they settled in. James Baker, Jr. was born in 1674. In 1677, after Jamestown was burned during Bacon's rebellion and after the Chowanoac War ended, land in what is now eastern North Carolina was being offered for half the cost of land in Virginia. The young family decided to accept the offer and purchased their small farm near the Chowan River.

One of the biggest issues evident in these new colonies was the gentrification of landowners versus the promise of land to indentured servants and free Africans. Bacon's Rebellion saw tobacco prices plummet, taxes increase, and large landowners subsidized by the Virginia government. The government wanted peace with the natives, whose land was promised to the indentured servants after their debts were paid. Nathaniel Bacon and others fought the Indians for their land while the government stood by doing nothing to help the commoners. Eventually, Bacon and others sought help from Governor Berkley. Berkley did nothing. So, Bacon and his followers burned Jamestown in 1677. Trouble continued late into the year until Bacon died suddenly and Berkley hung twenty of the rebels.

This incident is said to be the precursor to the American Revolution; taxation without representation. It also served as the catalyst for the end of indentured servitude and the beginning of the wholesale slave industry in Africa.

IN 1678, JONATHAN BAKER MOVED HIS FAMILY ONTO A SMALL homestead with his son. Jonathan, his wife Elizabeth, and younger son William (James's brother), along with James, Margaret, Jem, and their newborn daughter Katherine, needed a house large enough to accommodate two families. They used the abundant forest, and with the help of an adze and a large plane, were able to hew the logs for a much better fit rather than using rough logs. The house had four bedrooms, a great room, two fireplaces, and a large kitchen. The dining table was large enough to fit twelve people around it. The house was as sturdy as any house in any city. There was also a barn and a nice privy outside of the house. There was always activity on the homestead. The family were lively and happy.

True to his word, in five days Skiko appeared at dusk on the edge of the clearing with Kisis in tow. Jonathan saw Skiko first and hesitantly called to James. James came around the side of the barn, and seeing Skiko, yelled a friendly greeting and motioned them forward. Skiko carried a large bundle into the house.

Hearing the greeting, the rest of the family came out to see what was going on. James introduced Skiko and Kisis to his family, and they were warmly greeted after they had heard the stories told by James, and especially Jem. Skiko and Kisis were invited to join them for supper.

Skiko was amazed by the construction. He felt the logs and looked at every beam and wall. He took a special interest in the fireplaces, which were both burning.

Sitting at the table, he motioned to James, extending his forearms up with fists clenched, showing approval of the construction of the house. James nodded his thanks, and they began to eat.

Margaret and Elizabeth served the meal, but they were more interested in watching Jem and Kisis than anything else. Jem and Kisis sat together, motioning back and forth, giggling, and enjoying each other's company.

At first, the conversation was strained given the non-communication with the visitors. After watching Jem and Kisis carry on, the conversation picked up with the usual banter and fun that accompanied most meals. They all teased Jem, who took it in stride.

Skiko took it all in. He realized these people were no different from his family, enjoying each other's company while eating. He laughed several times, understanding the ribbing of Jem and motioning to Kisis in the same manner. Everyone understood his intention, and they also ribbed her. Eventually, Jem and Kisis left the table and went into the other part of the room, trailed by the table's laughter.

After dinner, Jonathan, Elizabeth, James, and Margaret sat with Skiko. He motioned to Margaret that he enjoyed the meal. It was the first time he ever had bread the way Jonathan had baked it. Jonathan was able to secure some flour in the settlement at Queen

Anne's Creek. He traded his baking abilities for it. Skiko rubbed his stomach to show his approval. Then he went over to the door and brought the bag he had carried in with him. Inside were sweet potatoes, which he motioned that they would plant in the morning. All understood and James thanked him.

Margaret and Elizabeth went to the barn and made a nice bed for Skiko and Kisis using straw and blankets. Skiko again thanked them in his way.

The next morning, Skiko and Kisis were up at dawn with everyone else. They were invited into the kitchen again and were offered breakfast. Jem sat at the table with an open book to begin his lessons for the day. Margaret had insisted on educating her son since she was educated herself. Kisis sat next to Jem and looked at the book he had opened. Margaret motioned to Skiko that she knew how to write, by penning in the air, and that she knew how to read, by opening her palms and looking into them. She then motioned to Jem that she was teaching him to write and read. Skiko watched Kisis, as she was engrossed in the book and the writing on the paper Jem had next to the book. She motioned to his pencil, and Jem let her write a line on the paper. She was amazed.

Skiko watched his granddaughter intently. Margaret motioned to Skiko that she could teach Kisis as well. He smiled broadly and nodded his head in agreement. He said, "Good." They both laughed.

James, Jonathan, and Skiko went to the adjoining field where some vegetables had been planted. Skiko found a large stick and started rubbing it in the dirt to clear the vegetation and dig a rut to plant. James held up a finger and told him to wait. He went into the barn and came back out with a large hoe. Skiko nodded in agreement and used the hoe to clear a line thirty feet long by one foot wide. He was impressed with how good a job the hoe did. James knew Skiko was probably using primitive tools and decided to give the hoe to Skiko. He had more and could get more.

After the ditch was dug, Skiko removed a pouch that, once

opened, smelled horrible. He motioned the contents were ground-up fish remains mixed with dirt and some other plant herbs. He sprinkled the mixture in the ditch and then took out the sweet potatoes. He showed them the eyes and how to cut the potato so that each section had an eye. One large potato gave six pieces, which were placed six inches apart and covered again with dirt. Skiko motioned that in four moons the crop would be ready.

After they were done, Skiko motioned that he had to leave, since it would take a long time to get back to his village. James talked to Margaret and Jonathan and decided he and Jem would take them back on horseback. He motioned to Skiko that they would use two horses, they would ride double since the kids were small, and he and Jem would come back. Skiko agreed, and they readied to leave.

Margaret and Elizabeth packed a lunch for them all and included enough bread for Skiko to have over top of what they would eat at lunch. He was grateful for their hospitality and James knew he would return the favor. James also gave him the hoe, which they had several more of.

James kept a vigilant eye on the route to Skiko's village. It was an easy ride on horseback given the flat plain of the country. Landmarks were plenty, and they made the trip to his village with no issues, making the trip in less than seven hours. Jem and Kisis rode on the backs of each man and rambled and motioned to each other the entire trip. James was amazed at how Jem had connected with this young girl with the lack of conversation. A bond was quickly developing between them.

THREE

When the travel party approached the village, dogs barked, and people came out to greet them. They saw James and Jem and were immediately on guard. Skiko rode a little ahead and yelled, "Cumay," (pronounced chu-may, which is "friend" in Algonquin). More people came out to see the visitors Skiko had brought, and the village came alive.

The village covered almost three acres of flat ground bordered by woodland on one side and a depression on the other. It was on a small plateau. All of the structures were surrounded by a stockade fence that was only five or six feet high. It was not really for protection but more to keep wild animals out. Inside the stockade fence, a series of small structures of bark huts, called wigwams, were arranged along the inside of the fence perimeter. They were well-kept and looked sturdy. There were five large structures that, in James's estimate, were meeting houses and buildings to store provisions.

Wigwam Village was drawn by Melanie Patxot.

Skiko led them to a wigwam where he and Kisis lived. There was no one there. However, several ladies from nearby wigwams came over and greeted them. Kisis jumped down and hugged one of the ladies, and then the others. She rambled on and they all laughed as she talked. Skiko smiled and offered James and Jem to come down and enter his abode.

The wigwam was a round dome with a hole in the top on one side for smoke to escape. It was constructed with very large branches sunk into the ground every five feet around the outside of the house, bent to the apex of the dome, and tied together. Inside those branches, smaller branches were placed about two feet apart, sunk into the ground, bent towards the apex of the dome, and tied together. On top of those smaller branches, bark from trees was placed as a shingle. The shingles completely covered the outside of the house. James didn't see the smaller frame until he entered the house. It was ingenious and created a warm environment.

One side of the house was a cooking area with a fire pit and grates to hang pots and other utensils on. On the other side, furs and skins were laid out as a sleeping area. The remaining area had furs and stuffed furs as pillows, arranged to sit on.

As they started to sit and relax, one of the women looked in and said something to Skiko. He motioned to James to follow him. They walked across the common area to one of the large longhouses situated nearest the common area. The longhouse was made in the same construction style as the smaller houses, with bent trees and bark. It was their council meeting house. They entered and were greeted by men sitting around the communal fire and waiting for their arrival. Skiko greeted everyone and introduced James. They sat to the left of the headman; James assumed. He was old and looked very weatherworn yet carried himself with authority. He looked at James, smiled, and then looked at another man about the same age as Skiko. There were no young men in the room, which James found odd.

The other man looked at James and said, "My name is Waya,

which means wolf. I know English. Only in tribe to speak good English."

James responded, "It is nice to meet you, Waya. Please thank Skiko and everyone else for welcoming me and my son to the village."

Waya relayed his message to the gathering, and they all shook their heads in agreement. "Skiko big man in tribe. His word big. You his friend a good thing," Waya said.

Skiko had brought the hoe with him to show everyone in the council house. They all took turns looking at it and then all began to speak to Waya at the same time. He listened to everyone in turn, and then answered back, looking at Skiko. Skiko nodded his head in agreement.

Waya continued, "Want to do trade with James. We give you hides, and you return with tools for plants."

James responded, "Agreed. First, I have a question. Where are all the young men? Are they out hunting?"

Waya looked at the others, mumbled James's question, hesitated, and then answered. The others lowered their heads and listened. "You know of war with your people?"

James said, "I was not here, but I heard of it."

Waya continued, "Long ago, Chowanoac people were very, very many. Many warriors. Your white people kept moving and taking lands of the Chowanoac and other tribes. Then came the pox. Many Chowanoac die from pox, and we went to war. White guns were too much for Chowanoac and many, many warriors died. Many warriors were sold into slavery. Skiko's son was sold into slavery by white men. His son's wife and Skiko's wife died of pox. Now he and Kisis are the only ones left in the family. Many other families the same. No young men left."

James was thoughtful, "I am very sorry for what happened. Please express that to your council."

Waya talked to them and explained what he had said. Skiko looked down.

James continued, "Please let everyone know I will do whatever I can to help your people. What do you want to trade and what do you want in return?"

Waya again talked to the council and was answered by several men.

"We have hides and furs to trade. We need blankets, planting tools, metal pots, knives, and guns."

James answered, "I can get you everything except the guns. They are very hard to find and cost dearly."

Waya relayed the message to the council, and they were all in agreement. Skiko talked, and they all listened intently to what he was saying. There was some discussion, but James knew Skiko was making a point, which they all seemed to respect. He then looked at Waya and asked him to translate.

"Skiko knows I am the only talker of English in our tribe. He says Jem's mother is a..."

James helped him finish, "Teacher?"

"Yes, teacher. Can she teach Kisis English tongue?"

James enthusiastically answered, "Yes, she can. Kisis will have to come back and live with me. Is that good?"

Waya translated. Skiko answered, "Skiko say Kisis stay one moon and you bring back."

James answered, "Tell Skiko I will bring her back in one moon along with the trade goods I get. When we come back, Jem can stay here for one moon to learn your language and customs. That way we will all be able to communicate through them."

"Communicate?" Waya pondered.

"Talk. We'll all be able to talk to each other," James responded.

Waya translated, and they all showed their approval and began talking at once. Skiko looked at James, smiled, and nodded his approval. Then he took out the loaf of bread Jonathan had given him and passed it around. They all loved it.

When they left the longhouse and went back to Skiko's house, the neighboring women were preparing supper for them. Skiko yelled, or really whooped, and Kisis and Jem came running up to the house. They were dirty, had briars in their hair and clothing, and were laughing at each other. Skiko looked at James and shook his head. James shook his head also, and both began to admonish the youngsters, who didn't really care. The women laughed at the young ones, too. They all sat outside and ate a meal of venison stew and a kind of bean bread that was delicious. Skiko then lit a pipe, and they smoked. James thought that Skiko's life was not really that bad if this was the best part of it. Life is hard. Everyone needs to accept and enjoy the good times that present themselves. They don't happen often and need to be relished. Life doesn't get better than a warm fire and a smoke after a good meal.

The next morning, two travoises were attached to the horses loaded with pelts. Kisis cried when saying goodbye to her grandfather and her neighbors, but once they started on their way, she became less sad and again bantered with Jem. James was on one horse and the kids were on the other, with James leading the other horse. At one point in the trip, James stopped and scolded both of them for spooking the horse with their nonsense. They settled down and were soon home.

That night at the dinner table, James and Jem recounted everything that had happened. Jonathan would go with James into town to trade the pelts. He knew most of the inhabitants because of his baking skills. Margaret figuratively took Kisis by the hand to make sure she was secure with her surroundings and felt comfortable. Kisis slept with Jem's young sister, Katherine. Every morning, they would have lessons.

FOUR

The next couple of days were eventful. James and his father took the pelts into town and were amazed at how quickly they sold and how much they received from them. In turn, they purchased hoes, axes, knives, several adzes, two planes, and four large cooking kettles, among other items.

While in town, Jonathan was approached by several of the town leaders to establish a bakery in the town, which was growing quickly. In 1680, the town was the largest in the colony that eventually became North Carolina. They needed services that would support the growing trade business from the port activity as well as the land made available by charter. More and more people moved into the area and the availability of flour made a need for a baker. Jonathan was happy with James on the farm. However, in several months, events would change his thinking.

Once home, it was life as usual for the men. Margaret, on the other hand, was now tasked with teaching a six-year-old how to read and write in a different language. She started Kisis out with the ABCs, their pronunciation, and how to write them. She also tutored Jem where he was with his studies and they eventually caught up to each other; both were only beginners.

Margaret was amazed at how intelligent Kisis was. She was able to understand and pick up the letters and numbers quickly and efficiently. When she did make mistakes pronouncing letters, Jem would laugh, and Kisis would turn to him, her eyes wide, jaw set and moving slightly back and forth. Margaret got to know that look. So did Jem. Margaret knew to let her cool down, but Jem would antagonize her; they would both almost come to blows. Several times Margaret had to physically restrain Kisis from belting Jem. She would grab her shoulders, make her look into her eyes, and shake her head back and forth. One evening, Jem had come to the dinner table with a bruise on his cheek. Margaret looked at Kisis and shook her head back and forth. Kisis just looked at her with a slight smile and nodded.

Within three weeks, they were both spelling and writing small words: dog, hat, sun, and other three-letter words that were easy to comprehend. Kisis could not get enough. She wanted more. Jem wanted to run around outside and play in the woods. It was a typical childhood for these two youngsters.

When it was time to take Kisis back, they loaded the two travoises with all of the supplies. Kisis begged Margaret to come back with her. So, she decided to make the trip with them.

Once in the village, everyone came out to greet their friends and to see Kisis. She was now somewhat of a celebrity, given her opportunity to learn the new language.

Margaret was at first hesitant. However, after seeing Skiko and experiencing the warmth and friendliness of the people, she relaxed and was quite taken aback by their charm. She gave him several loaves of bread, and he gave her a big smile back. They were fed, and afterward, the men gathered in the longhouse and looked at the tools James had brought. They were all very satisfied and decided to continue with their business dealings. More furs were brought in, and a list of items was given to James by Waya. This time they asked for blankets, cloth, sewing needles and thread, and other household-type items. And, of course, there was another request for guns.

James knew that Jem would be spending a month with them. So, Jem was brought into the council house and was introduced to all the men sitting there. He repeated each of their names and was made to feel comfortable with all of them. His task was to learn their ways and, hopefully, learn the language. It was intimidating for a six-year-old to leave his family for a month. But Kisis did it, and if she could do it, Jem made up his mind that he could do it too.

The furs were again loaded on the travois. As James and Margaret were leaving, Jem teared up and Margaret had second thoughts. She motioned to James, who also looked back, and he yelled to Jem; they would see him soon. He waved and stood there a good thirty seconds, watching them go. Then Kisis pushed him and he chased her through the village.

After four weeks, James and Jonathan made the trip back to the village with the merchandise requested by Skiko and the others. James had planted about an acre of the sweet potatoes and he informed Skiko the plants were growing well and would soon be harvested. Skiko showed him where they had planted and their crop, which was also doing well.

Eventually, Jem showed up in the village and neither man could believe what they saw. He was wearing only leggings and a loincloth, sunburned, bare-chested, and his blonde hair was unruly and full of briars. They both thought he had grown an inch or so. Jem saw his father and rushed to him, giving him a big hug, and then his grandfather the same.

Kisis and some other boys were not far behind him. She said hello in English. Everyone laughed. She did not like being laughed at. Her fists formed and her jaw tightened and moved back and forth. Jem pushed her shoulder and said, "Kiki." It was his nickname for her, and he gave her a smile. She calmed down.

In the council house, James and Jonathan again talked to the elders, and a good relationship was formed. The items they had brought back were well received and the beginning of a business relationship took root.

Kisis once again returned with the Bakers and spent the next month with them, learning much more than Margaret could believe. She was speaking in sentences and communicated and learned words and phrases much quicker than Jem learned the Algonquin language. She was remarkable.

Several things happened during that time. The farm was doing well, given the growth of the sweet potatoes. They had planted less than an acre, but the yield was high and James knew he had stumbled onto something good. The crop sold quickly in town and was highly sought after, making a good profit for the farm.

One evening at dinner, Jonathan looked at James and Margarete and said, "The town needs a bakery. There is plenty of flour and supplies arriving frequently enough to keep the town supplied. I don't really want to open a bakery, just getting out of one. But the town elders know of our dealing with Skiko and his people, and if I don't open the bakery, they will force us off of the farm."

Elizabeth frowned and said, "We will have to move into town and take William with us as an apprentice. It will leave you shorthanded here, James. But we see no other way."

James said, "I understand and we will get by. We can also help at a bakery during the winter. We are all in this together."

Jonathan, Elizabeth, and William moved into town and opened a bakery. It turned out to be successful, with Jonathan and Elizabeth buying property and eventually building a nice house in town.

FIVE

On Jem's sixteenth birthday, the Bakers held a get-together for the family with some close friends in town, and Skiko and some of their close Chowanoac friends. For the last eight or nine years, they had all been traveling back and forth between the village, the farm, and the town. The natives were still not quite welcome in town by some of the older citizens who were involved in the war, but most people accepted them, especially Skiko, who was somewhat of a diplomat.

James was now farming close to thirty acres of sweet potatoes. He had purchased a plow and employed the Chowanoac as laborers. The deal they had was to split the profits, so the Chowanoac were able to subsist on more than just hides. The hunting was getting scarce and the further west they hunted, the more they ran into Tuscarora and Cherokee hunters, their long-time enemies. They all knew a year's worth of hides would fetch around thirty pieces of eight. One slave fetched that much, or more. They had to avoid the hunts to stay safe. They made a good arrangement, and Skiko led his people into that form of subsistence.

Waiting for their friends to arrive, James asked Jem to climb the large pine to see if he could see anyone approaching. Jem scrambled up the tree in seconds and they were all amused at how quickly he navigated the tree. He was strong, almost six feet tall, and muscular from the farm work and the activities he partook in, especially climbing. He loved to hide in trees from Kisis and surprise her by jumping down and scaring her. She would howl and chase him until she caught him; she was a faster runner. She would tackle him with a leg scissor, taught to her by Skiko, which immediately brought Jem down. Then she'd playfully smack him around the head. Jem had her teach him that scissors move because there was no defense against it.

The town friends were already there when the Chowanoac arrived. They all greeted each other warmly and all the women started to prepare the food. Most of the native women learned some English, thanks to Kisis, and were able to chat amicably while preparing the food. Kisis held back, watching for Jem to ambush her. She was just coming to the clearing when Jem pounced on her and they rolled in the leaves until, employing the scissor takedown, she ended up on top of him, pinning his arms to the ground. They both relaxed and hesitated. Jem felt something he had felt before. It was not a new feeling, and he knew to relax. She felt the same, looking into his eyes and knowing each other's thoughts without even trying. The momentary hesitation subsided, and they both got up laughing. As they walked together into the clearing, the women stopped what they were doing and watched them, all smiling and looking at each other, knowing what was happening. But they never spoke of it. They also knew how difficult it was for these two young people to bear the scrutiny of others. Interracial relationships were highly frowned upon and only accepted by those close to and who intimately knew the couple.

The day was filled with fun and good humor. The harvest was coming along well. The men talked about it and were happy with the arrangement, knowing they could survive winters with enough food to feed the entire tribe. They had set up a small camp near the farm so they could work and not have to travel back to their village after a hard day's work.

At dusk, the day was drawing to a close and the festivities winding down, Jem and Kisis snuck away to go swimming in a small stream about a mile from the farm. It was their favorite swimming hole, and few people knew of its whereabouts.

It was dark, but there was a full moon. They swam and jostled, and Jem went and lay on the bank, watching Kisis swim for a bit until she got out of the water. She was wearing a sheer cotton shirt. As she came up the bank, her dark, small nipples protruded from the shirt, causing Jem to get hard immediately.

In the moonlight, she was beautiful. Long black hair was neatly combed. She had high cheekbones, a thin face with a firm jaw, and her penetrating eyes were black. She was thin, muscular, and about five inches shorter than Jem, but was still tall for her people. Her breasts were medium size and firm, and her hips were the same.

She noticed his erection. Without saying a word, she took off her shirt and undergarment and stood before him naked for the first time. She had watched Jem's eyes in the past and knew he wanted her as much as she wanted him. Jem got up, took off his clothes, and they erotically embraced for the first time.

They explored each other's bodies, not really knowing what to do. But they were so close, and their thoughts were so much the same, no words had to be passed between them to proceed. Jem was large, and Kisis was quite hesitant, not really knowing what to do.

Jem looked at Kisis. "Are you ready for this?"

Kisis said, "I have been wondering how long it would be before you took me. As always, I had to make it happen."

Jem chuckled. "I really don't know what to do."

"Neither do I," she said softly. "Let's just go slow."

Jem laid her back on the grass. He caressed her breasts, feeling and running his fingers over her erect nipples. She let out a small groan. He caressed her whole body, wanting to feel it for the first time; her abdomen, her thighs, her rear end, and finally, spreading her legs, he mounted her, entering slowly and with the awkwardness of a teenager. Kisis responded with a low guttural moan, a heavy intake of rattled breath; but eventually, she relaxed. They went slowly at first until Jem couldn't hold back. His motions increased in urgency until he exploded inside her. She moaned with soreness and delight.

They laid back, holding each other, and began exploring each other's bodies with soft caresses. They did this for about a half hour until Jem got hard again. She wanted to feel his manhood as she never touched one. She couldn't believe it and caressed him until he released before he was able to enter her. She watched in amazement and they both laughed. Instead of smacking him all over his head, as she usually did, she kissed him all over his head, something she would do for the rest of their lives.

When they returned to the farm, everyone was gone. The party had ended, and everyone was asleep, except for Margaret, who probably knew what had happened by Jem's quiet entry into the house and his immediate slumber.

The next morning, Jem woke with a start, seeing daylight much brighter than he was used to. He dressed and went into the kitchen, seeing his parents, Kisis, and Skiko already sitting at the table. Kisis' head was lowered with her face somewhat hidden. She looked up at Jem with a look of love, terror, and joy, all at the same time.

Jem sat down and his mother gave him a maternal look that he knew, as did his father.

Jem looked to Skiko. "Numohshomus (my grandfather), I love your granddaughter. It is our custom to ask for your permission to marry her. I now ask for that permission, with the blessing of my parents. I have very little to offer you for her, only my horse."

Skiko answered, "Nooshis (grandson), I speak English for your parents. You are part of my family long time now. I know you feel for Kisis, and she feels for you. I need no offering. You have my blessing." Skiko then looked to James, "This hard. I give blessing, you give warning."

James looked at them. "Both of you, look at me.

Jem and Kisis both looked to James and Margaret. "This marriage has been anticipated for a long time. Do not think your mother and I (looking at Margaret, and then Jem) think otherwise? There is already talk in town about the two of you and some people frown on any type of coexistence with Skiko and his people."

He paused and let that set in.

James continued, "Know that you will have problems with people the rest of your lives, as well as any children you will have. There are no preachers in town or anywhere that will conduct a marriage ceremony. It just isn't done."

Kisis looked up enthusiastically, "We can get married at the village."

Jem became indignant, "Papa, I hear what you are saying, and I understand. The people in town know Kisis. She works for Grandpa in the bakery and is there at least four days a week. I don't see how anyone would think of her less."

James responded emphatically, "Jem, that is where you are mistaken. They may know her, and they may like her, but she is beneath them in their eyes."

Skiko added, "I walk in town and people know me. They do not trust me and look down on me."

Jem said, "Mama, you have taught all of us the meaning of having an education and thinking for ourselves. I really don't care if we are married in town by a preacher or in the village. God knows how I feel about Kisis. That is enough for me."

Immediately, Kisis chimed in, "And I feel the same about Jem."

James continued, "I understand and agree with you both. Know that your cohabitation will not be tolerated in town, and you will have to stay here on the farm. Do you both understand the bigotry and scrutiny you will be under?"

They both nodded their heads. They understood their livelihood and daily life would be in the crosshairs of unruly people bent on dominating those whom they feel are inferior. Such is life, time immortal. Those who have the money, power, and influence will always try to keep it at the expense of those they intimidate and control.

The ceremony was held in the Chowanoac village with the Baker family in attendance. There was James and Margaret, with Jem's sister Katherine, Jonathan, and Elizabeth, along with James' brother William. It was a simple ceremony. It was held outside with the entire tribe attending. The bride and groom dressed in handmade clothing. The official was the pipe carrier, who said a few words to affirm their commitment. He then blessed them with the four winds, fire, and water. Each then made a commitment to the other as husband and wife. They then smoked from a pipe.

It was done. The celebration began. Food items for the feast included bread made by Jonathan and William, venison, squash, beans, corn, sweet potatoes, and sweets baked by Margaret. The bride and groom then gave away small handmade gifts to everyone in attendance.

The festivities ended in the afternoon and the Bakers, with the newlyweds, left for the farm. The couple retired to their new abode with good wishes from everyone. Their new home was an addition to the barn made livable by some recent renovations. It was warm, comfortable, and cozy, and they both loved it.

They had to be roused several days later, with empty food bowls outside of their door, with Skiko threatening to break them up.

Events took place in the next couple of days that changed everyone's life forever.

Six

During the golden age of piracy, roughly 1680 through 1725, the Carolinas were a favorite stop for first privateers, and then pirates, to sell their cargo and then resupply their ships with needed provisions. Privateers were privately owned boats commissioned by one government or another, that issued papers regarding their employment as privateers. They were sanctioned pirates, able to capture and sell opposing ships for prize money and whatever other income they could derive from the sale of the cargo, and even the sale of captured ships. The British government didn't have enough warships to fight the many countries they always fought. Privateers were an easy way to increase their presence in most waters. Once wars were settled, if privateers continued to raid shipping without a commission, they were considered pirates.

The town on Queen Anne's Creek was the largest and busiest port in the Carolinas in 1690. It eventually became the first capital of North Carolina.

Kisis was helping in the bakery when word came that two privateers were approaching the port. They were working frantically since they knew the bread and sweets would sell quickly to the crews coming into town. Jem's uncle William had expanded the bakery business to include dry goods and other items not sold by any other business. They would also need to purchase any goods the captains of the ships would have for sale, such as flour or molasses and other dry goods. The entire town was excited when the ships came to port, never knowing what exotic items they may have for sale.

The warehouses were owned by Dexter Hill, the wealthiest citizen in the town. He controlled most of the town property and rented space to any newcomers. He was connected to the Lord Proprietors of Carolina and wielded great power and influence. His oldest son, George, managed the warehouse and was a headstrong bully. He was in his early thirties and usually walked around town with an entourage of friends.

The two ships disembarked their goods and crews, and chaos reigned in town for two days. After provisioning their ships, they left as quickly as they had arrived. Word had come that a British Man of War was set to arrive in a day or two from Virginia.

The British Man of War usually carried up to 1000 crewmen on each ship. These ships carried more able crewmen than pirate ships. However, two pirate ships would have fewer crewmen and would spend much more during their leave in town. The officers on the Man of War tempered their sailors, and they behaved much better and spent much less than the crews of the pirate ships. They purchased everyday merchandise that William supplied, such as cloth and sewing implements.

William had asked Kisis to go to the largest warehouse and fetch supplies they would need. He asked her to take a young boy, Ben, with her to help carry items. Ben was the son of a slave owned by the Alsop family. He liked hanging around the bakery; he would run small errands in return for sweets. The warehouse was located along the waterfront. The front of the warehouse contained normal items, but the back sections contained many items the pirates had sold them from different parts of the world.

The British knew colonists would purchase and not pay tax on these items. The colonies were required to purchase all merchandise from their British Lords overseas. So, when pirates came along the coast and offered items for sale, the colonists did not have to pay taxes on that merchandise and usually paid less than they would normally pay for the same items from the British. This incensed the British, which is why they had the Navy make frequent stops and inspections at ports along the coast. The colonists loved the pirates. They also knew to keep the British Navy at arm's length and to hide whatever contraband they had.

Kisis and Ben entered the front of their warehouse. Jem was helping in the back rented space of the warehouse to accommodate new inventory. Kisis went to the front section William was renting. She grabbed a sack of sugar they would need and gave it to Ben, who was too small to carry the heavy sack. She chuckled. She said smiling, "Ben, that sack is almost as big as you."

"I can do it, missy," he said struggling with the sack.

"Just set it in the corner for now. We have other items to get."

As they were looking through some of their products that were in their section of the warehouse, George Hill and two friends walked through the front door. They immediately saw Kisis and approached her.

"Well, if it isn't the haughty little Indian girl," he spewed.

His two friends let out guffaws. Kisis whirled around and stood frozen for the moment. George approached within two feet of her. Her jaw clenched and moved from side to side, her fists ready.

"Where's your half-breed boyfriend, that Indian lover? He's not here to share you. Why don't I show you what a real man is like?"

"Leave me alone, and back away," she said.

George continued, "Aw, that's not being nice."

George grabbed the front of her smock and she yanked away, tearing her shirt in the process. Ben saw what was happening, and he ran out of the front door towards the bakery. George approached her again, and she struggled. His two friends joined in jostling her around and she let out several yells.

Jem was in the back section working, and heard the commotion, recognizing Kisis's voice. He burst into the front and saw what was happening. Without hesitating, he grabbed the first man he could and punched him in the face, knocking him down. George saw him and tackled him to the ground. He and his other friend started hitting and kicking Jem as he lay on the ground. The third man got up and joined in.

Jem was quick. He was able to roll over and sidestep some of the punches. While they were still moving around him, he used the scissor kick to bring one of the men down. But George punched him in the face, temporarily stunning him. As the two men looked over the top of Jem, Kisis grabbed a kerosene lamp and struck George across the back of the head with the lamp, breaking the glass and spilling kerosene everywhere. George's head was severely cut by the glass, with a piece lodged extremely close to his eye. The kerosene spread onto the floor and into some hay. There was another kerosene lamp nearby that was lit, and Kissy attempted to grab that lamp to use on the other man. The other man slapped her arm, and she dropped the lamp, causing the surrounding area to catch fire immediately. Soon, the entire side of the warehouse was burning. The glass that had stuck in Georgia's head had severed a gash in his temple and his eyesight was blurred. At that point, with the warehouse burning, all of them stopped the fight and tried to put the fire out.

Seeing the smoke, some of the others working near the warehouse sounded the alarm and everyone in town came running to extinguish the flames. Part of the warehouse was burned, but the majority of it was saved due to the quickness of the people that were working in the warehouse itself.

Little Ben had run all the way up to the bakery to tell William what was going on. William and Jonathan had come running with a couple of other workers from the bakery. They saw the flames, opened the doors, and helped extinguish the fire before it got too far out of control.

Part of the warehouse was burned, a big loss given some of the products that were there waiting to be sold to the crewmen coming from the Man of War. The townsfolk were incensed, finding out how the fire had started and why it had started. However, George, being injured, had his two friends tell the story they were talking to Kisis and were attacked by Jem and were just trying to defend themselves.

Jem and Kisis both denied the entire story. But since there was a loss of property and an assault, and Kisis had swung the lantern, both were held by the local constable by order of the town counselor and Governor of the region, who resided in the town. It was the word of three men versus two young adults. Ben was a slave boy, and his testimony was not relevant nor asked for.

The governor and the town counselors decided to have a quick trial to resolve the issue, saying that the Man of War was pulling into the port. They wanted to make sure this was taken care of before the officers and men from the ship disembarked and entered the town. It was quickly decided that Jem and Kisis were the cause of the fire, the loss of property, and the assault on George Hill. Jem was sentenced to a prison camp and Kisis was expelled from the town forever. James and William both approached Dexter Hill.

James started, "Mr. Hill, I am going to make this quick. There were three adult men against a sixteen-year-old boy and a sixteen-year-old girl. I believe my son's story, but I know it is irrelevant."

Dexter Hill responded, "Those two sixteen-year-olds partially blinded my son and cost me hundreds of pounds in the destruction of property."

William shot back. "Your son is a bully, and I do know how the altercation must have begun. But that is beside the point. I run the bakery now and much of the product I bake comes from ships other than His Majesty's Ships. If you do not relax the burden of punishment, the officers on that ship will know what has been transpiring and you will be held accountable. And you'll lose a bakery."

Dexter Hill sat back a minute. He looked at the room and all the people in it, all citizens of the town. Servants, black slaves, and natives were not allowed to attend. He looked out the window and saw Skiko looking directly at him, burning a hole through him with his eyes. Just As quickly as he saw Skiko, men forced Skiko away from the window. Mr. Hill leaned over and conferred with his fellow counselors. Just then, the captain and several officers from the ship entered the room. They saw the smoldering warehouse and inquired as to the issue. Once explained, the captain agreed with the usual punishment of imprisonment and banishment. However, the counselors ruled, at the suggestion of Mr. Hill and the captain, that Jem either go to prison for five years or serve in the Royal Navy as a seaman for five years. Kisis would endure indentured servitude, at the pleasure of Dexter Hill, to repay the losses from the fire.

James and William were anguished at the thought of Jem in the navy for five years, but they could not argue further without losing everything they had built and losing Kisis forever. They all agreed to the terms.

James took Dexter Hill to the side after the proceedings were done. James said, "I will make sure Kisis serves you well and does what she is told. But know this, if you or your son abuse her in any way or mistreat her in any way, you will answer to me. And know that Skiko will have to be told what has happened. If he hears of any abuse, you will never see him coming."

Dexter Hill said, "Is that a threat, Mr. Baker?"

James coolly responded, "No, it is a promise." He eyed Dexter Hill up and down and slowly exited the room, with William by his side.

Kisis was released that day. However, Jem was now in the service of the Royal Navy and had to be kept incarcerated while the ship re-provisioned and was in port, a total of three days. James had talked the constable into letting Kisis see Jem and talk to him through the bars of the cell before he was taken to the ship.

"This is not fair. It is horrible. What do we do?" Kisis lamented.

"We do what we are told, Kiki. We play out our sentences and when I get back, we will leave this area forever and make our own life somewhere else."

"But that will be five years. That's a long time. How am I supposed to take care of Grandfather and stay at that man's house all the time? What will become of grandfather?" she asked.

"My papa will help. Go to him for anything you need or that grandfather may need," he said soothingly.

"I will. I'll make sure that he is somehow taken care of. I love you Jem. You come back, no matter what."

"Wait for me, Kiki. Wait for me."

And with that, Kisis kissed Jem through the bars and was led away. That was the last time she saw Jem before he was taken on board. Jem sat back in his cell and wondered how he would survive five years without her.

As she walked away, Kisis felt a stirring in her body and did not know how she'd survive five years without Jem.

SEVEN

Kisis walked from the dock to the bakery, where James, Margaret, Jonathan, Elizabeth, William, and Skiko were waiting for her. She went into the bakery. With tears in her eyes, she fell into Margaret's arms. The two women stood together for what seemed an eternity. Eventually, they broke apart, and all sat down at a table to discuss the future. Kisis looked to Margaret, "What am I to do? How am I going to work for those people for five years?"

James responded, "You must. It seems right now as though your world has collapsed. But you must get through it."

Margaret added, "We will be here for you."

Skiko had been silent. He looked at his granddaughter, and she knew his thoughts. She looked at him. "Who will take care of you? How will you live without me?"

Skiko said, "Don't worry about me. You do as you are told, and we will decide what to do when you are free. I don't understand what happened. But there is nowhere to go for us, or our people. You are the future and you must listen to James and Margaret."

"I have to move to the Hill's house tomorrow. How will I see you?" Skiko responded.

"We are working with James at the farm. I will be close and will visit the town when you are in town as well."

William added, "We'll figure out your work routine and when you run errands, we'll make sure Skiko is nearby."

The next morning Kisis reported to Dexter Hill, and he remanded her to the care of his household manager, also an indentured servant. Her name was Mrs. Alston and seemed to be a nice woman.

Mrs. Alston was in her early fifties, was tall, and seemed large. However, she was not overweight. She had a commanding presence that anyone would know she was in charge. She had long brown hair tied neatly into a bun and usually wore a kerchief tied around her hair, mostly when performing chores. During lunch and dinner service, the kerchief came off. She had large brown eyes, a round face, and a set jaw. When she spoke, people listened. She was direct but not blunt, the difference being her use of language that impressed Kisis immediately. She glided throughout the house, knew every nook and cranny of the house, and knew Mrs. Hill well. Mrs. Alston knew exactly what she demanded of the staff.

Mrs. Alston took Kisis to the top floor of the house and showed her where her room would be. Kisis had only a few personal items, and Mrs. Alston said she would be able to get her additional clothing for the chores she'd be doing. The room was tidy but very small, with a small bed and a poor mattress. It was definitely warm on the upper floor of the house. She then told Kisis what her chores would be, starting with the laundry. Listening to Mrs. Alston, Kisis realized she would be little more than a slave, earning wages that would go directly towards the cost of the damage to the warehouse. She wondered how she would get through this trial. And, knowing that George was in the house made her even more apprehensive.

She started washing, rinsing, and hanging the laundry. The good part was there were only three people residing in the house. The bad part was they had five additional indentured servants working for them, whom Kisis also had to do laundry. It was a daily job that took several hours each morning.

Toward late morning, she reported to the kitchen to help serve lunch. The cook was a mean man in his late fifties who looked at Kisis sideways every time she entered the kitchen. After a couple of stares back at him, he ended his glares. But he was mean and talked to her like she was second-rate, a native. Knowing the look and the attitude of others she had received in town, she went about her business and, much to his surprise, efficiently. From that first day on, the cook was still mean but also left her alone.

After the Hill's had their lunch and moved on with their day, the servants then sat and quickly ate their meal. The stable keeper/chauffeur was a man in his early thirties that was married and very nice, living with his wife above the stables. He spoke to Kisis cordially, already knowing her from working in the bakery. The gardener was a man in his late forties from Scotland who had a very deep voice and brogue, which was very hard to understand. He called her Missy, which was endearing to her, and she liked him from the start. He also lived above the stable in a different room than the chauffeur and his wife. The mean cook had his own room off of the kitchen area.

The only other servant was a young lady named Emilie in her mid-twenties, who was part of the household, taking care of all the duties required by Mrs. Alston. She looked at the teenage Kisis and gave her a big-sister smile. Her room was on the upper floor too, in between Kisis' room and Mrs. Alston's room.

After their lunch, Kisis and Emilie cleared the settings, washed and dried all the dishes, set the dining room for the dinner meal, and then were given duties in the parlor and the dining room. They cleaned rugs, cleaned furniture, dusted, and polished the brass.

In the late afternoon, they went back to the kitchen and helped with dinner service, which began at seven o'clock. After dinner, they cleaned the dining room and sat down for their own dinner, once the Hills retired for the evening. It was close to ten o'clock when the kitchen was cleaned and Kisis went to her room. She would be awakened at 5:00 a.m. by Mrs. Alston to start the next day.

That evening, around ten thirty, she heard a quiet knock at her door. She opened it to see Emilie standing there. She invited her in, and they sat on her bed and chatted. Emily had been there for several years and was willing to give Kisis advice on how to get through their situation.

Emilie said, "You will get used to the routine. It takes a couple of weeks but really isn't that bad. I have seen worse and know of those who work for much worse people. The Hills aren't that bad, except for George. Stay away from him, and inform Mrs. Alston if you have any problems with him. He is such a lout."

Kisis said, "He is the reason I'm here."

Emilie responded, "I already heard. What happened?"

Kisis began, "I went into the warehouse to get items for Jem's uncle at the bakery. George and his two buddies started to jostle me around. I yelled at them, and Jem heard me. He was working in the back of the warehouse. He came in and shoved one of George's buddies to the ground, and George and the other guy started beating up on Jem. They had him on the ground, punching and kicking him. I hit George with a lantern, which cut him really badly. He fell back, but the other two kept beating Jem. I grabbed another lantern and swung it at them. It was still lit, fell, and broke into flames. Jem got the beating, and we both got the blame for the fire."

Emilie said, "George hasn't come out of his room yet. I imagine he will be furious if he has any partial blindness or any scars. He is a bully and always has been. Believe me, I know. If it wasn't for Mrs. Alston, I would have been abused by him."

Kisis said, "He thinks he's a lady's man."

Emilie chuckled. "I know. He is not that attractive."

They both giggled and continued chatting for a while.

However, the days were long and hard, and they needed sleep. A friendship was developing between the two women.

Two days later, George came out of his room. Kisis was scrubbing the hallway floor as he came down the steps.

"You, Indian bitch. What are you doing here?"

Kisis indignantly responded, "You know exactly why I'm here. And I must say, that bandage around your head looks good on you."

George took a menacing step towards her just as Mrs. Alston came through the kitchen into the hallway.

"Glad to see you are up, Master George. Is there anything I can get you?"

George spewed, "You can get this bitch out of our house."

"Now, Master George," Mrs. Alston started. "You know why she is here, and you were told she would be here. If you have any issues with her, you come to me, understood?"

George sneered at Mrs. Alston and then at Kisis. He walked through the hall into the kitchen. Mrs. Alston watched him leave and then turned to Kisis. "You keep your distance from him. I know your temperament. Do not antagonize that man. He is violent and has fits of rage. Do you understand?"

"Yes, ma'am," she said.

"Promise me. I won't always be here to protect you. Avoid him at all costs," she ended.

"Yes, ma'am," Kisis said, accommodating her.

Of course, it was all just starting.

That night, Kisis was in her room reading from one of the two books she had brought with her. A soft rap at the door told her Emilie wanted to talk. She softly said to come in so as not to wake Mrs. Alston.

Emilie came in and saw Kisis putting down her book.

"You can read?" she asked, astonished.

"Yes, why?"

"I'm sorry. It's just that most women in our position do not know how to read, or write, for that matter. How did you learn?" Emilie inquired.

Kisis explained to Emilie her relationship with Jem, how they met, and how his parents and her grandfather had arranged for her to learn English and for Jem to learn the ways of the Chowanoac. She also told her about Margaret being a teacher and how she taught Kisis much more than how to read and write.

Kisis went on. "Jem is my soulmate. We grew up together, and his family is like mine, as my grandfather is like his grandfather. We both share each other's family."

Emily said, "Sounds wonderful. You must really love Jem."

"More than you can imagine," she ended wistfully.

Kisis kept her secret marriage to Jem to herself. She would not speak of it to anyone other than family. She knew problems would arise in town if that secret would become common knowledge. Everyone already knew how close she and Jem were. But to acknowledge their native marriage would create animosity to not only her but her families also, which she could not bear.

Emilie continued, "I was married once. It was in England. My husband was a good man, and I was deeply in love with him. We lived in a port town and were walking down our street one day when a conscription gang from the navy grabbed him and forced him onto a navy ship. Several months later, the ship was destroyed during the war and went down with all hands. I didn't know what to do. So, I signed on to come to the new world and seek my freedom here."

Kisis asked, astonished, "The navy just grabbed him off of the street?"

"Yes, they do it all the time. We are at war with France. If you don't have the social status or money to buy your way out, the people in power to do whatever they want," she stated as a matter of fact.

Kisis said incredulously, "That is not right."

"I know," Emilie mused. "But such is the world we live in. I was a domestic servant in England, which is all I know. I will probably end up doing this for the rest of my life."

"What will you do if you do get your freedom?" Kisis asked.

"I don't know yet. The Hills aren't people who will let their servants go. I'm not sure how or when it would happen. But I must ask you something?"

"What?" Kisis inquired.

Emilie asked sheepishly, "I cannot read or write. Can you teach me?"

Kisis thought for a minute. Then she looked at Emilie and realized the state she was in and what her future prospects were. Without any type of knowledge or wherewithal, she would be forced to maintain this kind of servile work for the rest of her life.

Kisis started, "OK. Here is what we'll do. Each night for a half hour, I'll teach you to read and write and to learn numbers. But I need books and paper for you to do this. I will write a note to William at the bakery. When you go for bread, take him the note and Margaret will get us everything we need. Hide the books and paper under the breadbasket when you return. Then we'll hide it all in here."

"Oh, you will do this for me?"

Kisis said, "Of course. But you just promise not to let anyone know what we are doing, especially Mrs. Alston. I'm not sure she'll look kindly on either one of us. And, in the note will be my request for more books for me to read, other than the two I have."

"I promise, Kisis. Thank you, thank you," she said while bowing her head into Kisis's hands. Emilie was almost crying.

Kisis thought to herself that she now had a reason to persevere, the ability to give back what she was given by the Bakers. And she would have a clandestine way to communicate with her family.

After Emilie left her room, Kisis again wondered how she would get by without Jem. Her stomach was in knots most of the time, almost to the point of nausea. She never ever had that feeling before. It was new to her.

EIGHT

J em was taken on board the *Coventry*, a British ship of the
line with over 100 guns and a crew of close to 1000 able
seamen. The ship was huge, with three masts and four sails
on each mast.

Jem was a landsman, a seaman with no sea experience. He was
the lowest ranking man of the crew, as well as the youngest crew
member, other than the cabin and powder boys. He was given over
to the bosun's mate in charge of below-deck operations. The
bosun's mate, Mr. Beasley, led him to steerage where he would
sleep and stow what little clothing he had. Most crewmen were
bunked under the forecastle, on the opposite side of the ship, which
had much more headroom and was open and airy. Steerage is
where the new crew stayed. It had low beams, which meant
crouching to walk, and it held some cargo and any animals kept for
food. Chickens, cattle, and sometimes pigs shared his berth. The
steerage was over the head, which most of the time reeked of
human waste.

Mr. Beasley informed Jem he would answer to only him and
the officers above his rank. He also informed him that any trouble
coming from him would involve the cat, the whip kept in a red bag

on the mainmast for punishment. The cat-o'-nine-tails, the cat, is believed to date back to ancient Egypt, where the domestic cat was sacred and, even then, was said to have nine lives. The belief is when beaten with cat hide that the victim gained virtue from the whip, part of the cat's nine lives. The navy cat had knots on the end that split the skin, and the punishment was usually administered by the bosun's mate on a British naval ship. When the "cat came out of the bag," someone was going to be flogged (which is where the expression 'cat's out of the bag' came from). Mr. Beasley gave Jem the impression he fancied using the cat. Jem thought he was off in the head.

Mr. Beasley told Jem at dusk he would be expected to be part of the first watch at four bells, 4:00 a.m. So Jem retired to his bunk under a huge beam in the corner of the steerage, the worst place to sleep. It was damp and smelled horrible.

In the next bunk, a man turned over and extended his hand. "Hello. I'm Billy Parker. Welcome aboard the *Coventry*."

"Jem Baker. Nice to meet you, Billy."

Billy went on, "If you need anything or any information, I'm your man."

Billy Parker, as Jem would find out, hailed from Portsmouth, England, the largest port in England at the time. It is on the south coast and is in proximity to London. Billy had entered the service at sixteen, just like Jem, and had been on a warship for over four years. His parents were dead and the sea life, like most men after two to three years of service, became his calling. He did have two older sisters in Portsmouth to whom he sent money as often as he could, as his pay came.

Billy was a little shorter than Jem and did not have the education Jem had. But he was intelligent with bright blue eyes, flowing blonde hair tied at the back as was customary of the time, and he had a bearing that Jem trusted immediately. He was as tall as Jem and as muscular as Jem, given his duty on the sails. Climbing rigging and ropes, hauling out canvas sails, and pulling up the canvas were hard and physical work. There were few duties on a wooden sailing ship that were not demanding work. Most sailors of the age were thin, wiry, and very strong. Billy's and Jem's heights were an exception to the norm.

"Thanks, Billy. I'm not sure what to do. I've never been on a ship before, let alone left home. This will be interesting, to say the least."

Billy added, "A word of caution. Mr. Beasley, who we call Beastly, is not to be trifled with. He gives out all cat punishments, and he loves it."

Jem responded, "I got that impression."

Billy continued, "Something else. All new men, especially young ones, he takes a fancy to. He'll be around later with his friends to try to make you his 'matey.' They are sick and take pleasure in raping the new guys, just like yourself. If you give in to him once, he'll always be around. Here, take this splint of wood. If he tries anything, put it to his throat and let him know you will not be a part of his sickness."

Jem looked at him, wide-eyed. "I thought it was illegal?"

"It is. But if no one ever comes forward, they continue with it. We are tucked away in steerage and can't be heard topside or by anyone who can do anything about it," Billy ended.

"Thank you for the advice, Billy."

Homosexuality was illegal in the Royal Navy, but it did happen. It was more common on privateer and pirate ships. The term *matey* was a common form of friendship used by all sailors. However, it was derived from the French term *Matelotage*, an agreement amongst pairs of sailors, in the 17th and early 18th centuries. It was an economic partnership. Matelots would agree to share their incomes and inherit their partner's property in the case of their death. They fought together, lived together, and shared everything. It was a form of insurance. Thought of as platonic, with the long voyages at sea without the company of women, some think it also had sexual implications. Others think homosexuality was common with men at sea for long stretches of time. It was definitely frowned upon by the Admiralty, which had strict regulations regarding homosexuality, and there was severe punishment for those found guilty of partaking in such activity.

Regarding Pirates, their written codes were the first of their kind resembling a democratic society. They spelled out what happened to a pirate's belongings if he/she was killed in battle or lost at sea. Each pirate designated a beneficiary if he was lost and captains made sure their wishes were granted. We know it today as the Pirate's Code. What they did personally mattered little to anyone else. Relationships were common among pirates, and most were left alone.

At 4:00 a.m., after a sleepless night, Jem was roused for his watch. Watches lasted four hours, and afterward, he would have breakfast. After breakfast, until his next watch at 4:00 p.m., Jem was assigned duties on the ship. With close to 1000 men on a ship, one would think there was not much to do. However, the wind, salty air, and the sea constantly eroded everything the ship was made of. Rigging, decks, sails, yards, halyards, pulleys, and anything iron had to be constantly cleaned, greased, repaired, or replaced. Most ships had a lead carpenter and a crew of twenty designated specifically to repairs. The same goes for a crew of up to twenty sailmakers and menders. There were cooks, stewards, navigators, cannoneers, and officers above every work detail. The ship was crowded and a beehive of activity.

After Jem's last watch, he would have supper, an hour or so of free time for mending clothes, reading, and then lights out at 10:00 p.m. That first day, he was exhausted, not knowing what he was doing, apprehensive of the ship and the sea, and not getting much rest prior to coming on board.

At 2:00 a.m., Jem was nudged awake by Beasley and two other men who stood over him. He looked over and noticed Billy was absent; he was on his watch.

"What do we have here, friends? This young lad looks as

though he could use some company," Beastly sneered through the dim light. He rubbed Jem's bare chest with the palm of his hand. The other two men stood at the opposite sides of his cot.

"He looks like he wants company. Let's touch him some more and see if he likes it," said one of the other men.

Jem quickly retrieved the splinter of wood under his pillow, and in a swift motion kicked both legs into the chests of the men who bent over him. He shoved Beasley back with his other arm. He hopped down and used the scissor move to subjugate Beasley and held the splinter to his throat. Jem hissed, "Move and you'll bleed out right here."

The other two men got their bearings but Beasley held his hands out, signaling them to stand down.

"I am not to be trifled with. Any more occurrences and all of you will have to sleep with one-eyed-jacks," (Sleeping with one eye open to watch for attackers) Jem hissed again.

"Okay, okay, matey," Beasley relinquished.

Jem released Beasley and got to his feet with his back to the hull, holding the splinter like a knife. One of the other men pulled out a knife and was about to lunge at Jem. Beasley's look kept him from attacking. "Stow it. Now is not the time." Then he looked at Jem menacingly. "You are mine and never forget it. You will rue the day you did this. Mark my words, someday you and me and we will violently part ways."

Jem never broke his gaze from Beasley and his men. They stared at each other for several seconds, and then the attackers backed out of steerage. They turned and silently went up on deck and returned to their berths under the forecastle deck.

Billy came down at four bells to rouse Jem and saw him awake, sitting on the end of his cot, holding the splinter of wood. He knew what had happened. "Beastly?" he asked.

"And two others," Jem answered. "But I got the better of them. They left quietly and very mad."

Billy said, "They'll have it in for you now. Be careful."

"I will," Jem answered resignedly.

Jem's 4:00 a.m. watch was uneventful. He was positioned over the stern castle near the helm. He was able to watch all comings and goings the entire length of the ship.

After his quick breakfast, Beasley sought him out for his day's duties. He was taken to the forecastle deck stairs and went down to the lowest deck of the ship, above the keel and on the deck above the bilge and ballasts. The bilge smelled horrible. At the very bow of the ship on that last deck was the head, below steerage. The ship was pointed at the front. On each side of the hull were ten benches with holes cut into them. This was the head of the ship where men relieved themselves. It was called the *head* because the wind was always behind the ship pushing it forward. The wind would take the smells out to sea in front of the ship rather than permeate the rest of the ship. The holes in the benches went directly into the sea. Next to each hole was a long, thick rope, about five inches in diameter, that was frayed at the end and dangled into the sea. When a sailor relieved himself, they would pull the rope up, clean themselves with the frayed ends, and then drop it back into the sea for its cleaning. Another method that was used at the time was to tie a heavy rag onto the end of a rope and dragged in the water for cleaning, the same as a frayed rope end. It was called a tow-rag. Hence, where the phrase "you little tow-rag" originated.

The entire crew used this head, except for the captain, the first mate, the quartermaster, or any prominent guest; they had a separate, private head near their cabins. Beasley explained that the head would have to be cleaned daily.

Beasley started, "This miscreant of a sailor will show you what to do." He pointed to another sailor. "I will inspect your work and God help you if it is not done properly. When you are done here, make sure the captain's head is cleaned. If he is not satisfied with it, you'll both pay with the cat."

Beasley left the head, and Jem looked at his workmate. They introduced themselves to each other. The sailor was African, but he spoke with an English accent. "Nat Cummings. Born in Guinea, raised in Guinea and in York."

"Jem Baker. Born in Carolina and raised in Carolina."

They both laughed at the subtle joke. Nat was light-skinned for someone from Guinea. Guinea had also been a trade crossroad for centuries. He was about five inches shorter than Jem and had rough hair and even rougher stubble, but not a beard. His eyes were bright and, like Billy, not educated. He was very intelligent and wise about the ways of the world. He and Jem, due to their work relationship, eventually became very close friends.

Jem could not believe what he was tasked with. He could climb a tree in an instant, thinking he might work on the rigging. Now, he would be cleaning the head.

Nat pulled out two long-handled brushes, which had stiff bristles. They scrubbed each bench in turn. Every two holes had a hinge that lifted. They lifted the hinge and scrubbed the top, bottom, and sides of each bench and as far down the hull as the brush would reach. They used a type of lye soap that somewhat cleaned any remaining particles. Then they lifted a large bucket on a long rope of seawater and rinse each section. The process sounded easy enough. However, each bench took time and there were constant interruptions by crewmen using the head.

The bucket of water was very, very heavy. Nat's defined chest and biceps from lifting that bucket every day did not go unnoticed by Jem. Jem's first attempt at lifting the bucket proved painful. He did it, but his muscles ached from the exertion.

Jem was assigned to head duty from that time on. He got used to lifting the buckets of seawater and his upper torso and arms began to bulge, just like Nat's. He was strong, and healthy, given the circumstances. When beaten to general quarters, battle-ready status, he and Nat were assigned to the lower gun deck to carry iron shot from the storeroom to the cannon crews. They worked alongside the powder monkeys, young boys assigned to that duty.

His daily routine did not change. He had stern deck watch from

4:00 a.m. to 8:00 a.m., breakfast, head duty until 4:00 p.m., stern watch from 4:00 p.m. to 8:00 p.m., and then a quick supper. Lights out at 10:00 p.m.

There were several helmsmen he became acquainted with during this duty. One, in particular, was an educated sailor whom he conversed with and discussed a range of topics. The man became Jem's tutor on seamanship, showing him how to read the stars, use a cross-staff, and steer the ship. The cross-staff, also known as Jacob's Staff, was a navigational tool, the precursor to the sextant. It was used to measure the angle between the horizon and a celestial body such as the sun or stars. By knowing this angle, a navigator could then determine his latitude and direction. Jem loved learning how to sail, much more than cleaning the head. They also traded books available on board.

The helmsman always steered the ship from the companionway. Jem stood on the poop deck, next to a navigator, and talk to the helmsman below. The poop deck originated from the French term 'la poupe.' It was the uppermost rear deck on the ship. The deck was elevated so as to see the entire ship before them and see the ocean in front of the ship. That raised rear deck, during foul weather, usually drenched the navigator and anyone else standing on that deck, from rain, waves, and wind. The term 'I'm pooped,' or tired from the elements, is where it originated.

Both the helmsman and the navigator had compasses in binnacles, which were glass-enclosed stands about waist high that kept the compass dry and protected from the salty air. They also had a compass on the bow deck as a backup in case battle would destroy any of them.

The helm was a long pole that was attached to a greased lever several decks below. Helm wheels were not invented until after 1703. Moving the helm left or right, through a slot in the floor, would move an identical pole several decks down. The pole would move a perpendicular piece of wood that was attached to the rudder. Moving the helm left in the companionway would move the matching pole right underneath, which would move the rudder left. So, a port (left) helm move would make the ship turn to port.

This technology is still in use today. When the wheel was invented, the pole below was replaced with a geared wheel, but the concept prevailed. It's also worth noting that the first ship wheels were doubled, needing two steersmen to move the wheel, since it was so hard to move. Some pictures of old ships show a double wheel.

On larger ships, the helm was only able to navigate about a fifteen- to twenty-degree turn. The sails on the masts were on swivels that could be turned about five degrees. So, a ship making a sharp turn for an attack would only be able to realize, at the most, a twenty-five- to thirty-degree turn. If you picture a modern speedboat that has modern motors and rudders, they still are only capable of making about a sixty-degree turn without capsizing. The difference is that wind and the sea made the wooden ships much harder to navigate when making turns. An experienced sailing master at that time was a critical member of any captain's crew.

Jem took all of this in and loved the technology of the ship. He was a quick learner and the men on his watch enjoyed his company.

Several times, while cleaning the captain's head, Jem saw the captain and once bumped into him, literally. He excused himself profusely while the captain stood there amused. The captain told him no worries and to just keep his head clean. Jem responded he gladly would, doffing his cap.

Mr. Beasley watched Jem like a hawk. He waited for Jem to make a mistake so he could use the cat on him. But Jem steered clear of him for a very long time. Mr. Beasley had other victims to deal with.

NINE

Kisis had been working at the Hills for over four weeks and had grown accustomed to the routine. Her work became easier as she made it her goal to accomplish each task to the best ability. Mrs. Alston was very pleased with her and made sure the Hills were aware of the quality of her work.

She tutored Emilie almost every night and made progress with her. Emilie was a quick learner with letters and writing, but she excelled with her numbers. Emilie had a good grasp on money, which made the numbers much easier to learn.

Kisis had bumped into George several times. Each time he spewed snide remarks while she bit her tongue. One morning, he cornered her in the barn as she was fetching milk and eggs. "You miss that boyfriend of yours yet? You know he'll never return, don't you?" he sneered.

Nonchalantly, Kisis said, "Please excuse me. I have to deliver these to the cook."

"You will get lonely. And when you do, I'll be here to satisfy you. I'll make you howl with delight," George spat.

"I don't think so. Please let me by." Kisis tried to move around him, but he blocked her way. Just then, he grabbed her breast, twisting the nipple as he let go. She swiped at his hand, and he backed up slightly and laughed. She backed further away and stood in a way he knew she was ready to spring on him.

Kisis sneered at him. "I can open that cut on your face easily and quickly. Touch me again and you'll have a large scar for life. Not many women like men with large scars."

George backed up and instinctively covered his face. She moved around him quickly and exited the barn.

As she left, she heard his guttural voice. "You, Indian bitch. You'll get yours. Someday you will come to me willingly."

Her stomach twisted in knots. She felt woozy and thought she was going to wretch. Around the side of the house near the kitchen, she stopped and leaned on the house, holding her stomach. She threw up what little was in her stomach. Her face flushed and her knees wobbled.

Mrs. Alston watched this from the kitchen window. As Kisis entered the back door, Mrs. Alston stopped her in the alcove so as not to be heard. She whispered, "What is wrong? You look like you are going to faint."

Kisis said, "I don't know. I haven't been able to eat for several days."

Mrs. Alston looked long into Kisis' face. "Have you had your time of the month yet?" she asked.

"No," Kisis responded. "I'm two weeks late."

"Honey, you are with child," Mrs. Alston stated as a matter of fact.

"I can't be. What am I going to do?" Kisis asked with a sob. She looked at Mrs. Alston and didn't quite know what to expect from her. "What will happen with the Hills? Will they force me away?"

Mrs. Alston softened somewhat and looked at Kisis. "This happened prior to you starting to work here. If the father is that boy you had the fight with, I'd say go to his parents and work through this with the Hills. Some arrangement will have to be made."

Kisis looked at her appreciatively and said, "If I do that and stay here, will I be able to do my work for you? You have my word that I will work hard and not back down on any job given to me, until a time when I won't be able to."

"Deal," said Mrs. Alston. "I had two children while working, and it can be done. But once you get seven to eight months in, things will change. You can't possibly work at that time."

She continued, "On Sunday after the meal, you go and see your family at the bakery. I'll make sure he stays and waits for you."

Kisis said, "On Sundays, he and his parents usually go to Jem's farm for dinner with his brother. Please ask them to have dinner in town Sunday, and I'll go to them in the evening."

It was arranged. Kisis and Mrs. Alston sent a note with Emilie to William, and he sent word back they would all be there Sunday evening at Jonathan and Elizabeth's house. He asked Emilie what was going on. But she didn't know and couldn't help him. Emilie told Kisis that William was chatting with her much more than normal. She wasn't sure whether he was trying to get information out of her or whether he just wanted to spend extra time talking to her.

Emilie was average height and slim with slim hips. In a normal dress, her figure was very appealing. What made her attractive was her congenial expression that would disarm any man at any time. She had large green eyes and long auburn hair, with red highlights abundant in sunlight. Her face was thin, and her eyes were inset into her high cheekbones. Her origins were definitely Celtic.

Emilie liked William very much. Kisis smiled and said he was a very good person, like an uncle to her, which he was.

Every Sunday the help was free in the late afternoon, a couple of extra hours than the normal workday. The prior Sunday, Kisis had to finish some work that she didn't finish Sunday morning. So, she hadn't seen anyone for two weeks. Since Emilie liked William, she asked her to come along to meet everyone and to see if

William was interested in her. Besides, Emilie would find out soon enough about Kisis's pregnancy.

They quickly finished their Sunday chores after the meal, and by three o'clock they were hurrying along the main street toward the bakery and the Baker house, which was only 100 yards from the bakery.

When the door opened, everyone was there to greet her, including Skiko. Introductions were made to Emilie, and Kisis watched William smooth his hair and press his shirt closer into his trousers. She knew right away.

As the greetings died down, Kisis approached Margaret, and while hugging her she whispered, "I need to talk to you."

Margaret frowned and they went into the kitchen for privacy. Kisis whispered, "I'm in somewhat of a bind."

Margaret looked at her quizzically and asked, "What is it? I'll help if I can."

Kisis rubbed her stomach. "I'm pregnant."

Margaret let out a yell of joy and everyone stopped talking in the other room. She led Kisis into the living area and all eyes were on her.

Margaret looked at James and smiled, "You're going to be a grandfather." She looked at Skiko and said, "You're going to be a great-grandfather."

Kisis looked at Skiko and thought he was going to cry. She hugged him and he held her tight. The rest, after getting over the shock, all gathered around her and congratulated her.

Emilie smiled and said, "I'll take care of you, don't worry."

Kisis answered, "Mrs. Alston was the one who told me I was pregnant. She knows and told me she'd take care of me too."

Dinner was lively, and Kisis was reminded how much she missed everyone. Then she thought of Jem and how he'd miss the birth of his child. She almost began to weep.

After dinner and when things settled down, William found a

corner with Emilie. James and Margaret, Jonathan and Elizabeth, and Skiko sat around the table talking.

Kisis said, "Jem will miss the birth of his first child."

James interjected, "We know. The issue at hand right now is how to get you time when you are due and time after the birth so you do not have to be at the Hills."

Margaret said, "You'll need a month before the birth and probably two after the birth to recover and be with your child."

Kisis said, "Will the Hills go for that?"

Jonathan spoke. "I will deal with Dexter Hill. We will offer him payment for your absence. That will accomplish two things. One, it will force him to come up with an amount owed by you for the damage. Then we'll be able to figure out, through your pay, how long it will take to pay the debt off. That way, they won't be able to keep you indefinitely."

James added, "That is right. Those people never put an amount of pay towards debt, since most indentured servants can't read or write. By law, they have to. But most of the people in power bend the laws in their favor. This will force Hill to say what her debt is and what her pay is, so we can figure out how long it will take her to pay it off."

Kisis chimed in, "Look at Emilie. I am teaching her to read and write. She has been with the Hills for two years and has no idea how much her passage from England costs or how much she is in debt to the Hills. She literally could be there forever."

Jonathan added, "We'll look into her situation also if you'd like us to."

"Please do," Kisis finished.

They all looked at Emilie and William in the next room.

Kisis said, "She really likes William, and I think he likes her too. That is why I asked."

Jonathan looked at Skiko and shook his head. "I'm getting old. I can't keep up."

Skiko smiled. Elizabeth put her arm on Jonathan's shoulder.

"You *are* getting old. Just worry about the bakery and we'll take care of everything else." They all laughed.

ON TUESDAY, JONATHAN, JAMES, AND WILLIAM ARRANGED A meeting with Dexter Hill. They met at his office, and his son George attended the meeting.

James began by saying Kisis was pregnant with his grandchild. They'd like to come to an arrangement with him.

George let out a guffaw. Mr. Hill reprimanded him immediately. "George, that's enough."

George responded, "I knew your boy was an Indian lover. And so are the rest of you."

Again, Mr. Hill said, "George."

James began, "Mr. Hill, for many years now I have done business with the Chowanoac. They are now subsistent farmers, as I am. They are not a threat to you or anyone else. But Kisis is the granddaughter of Skiko, a prominent Chowanoac, who is also my good friend. She and my son Jem were married in a native ceremony. Since no preacher would marry them here and the law forbids intermarrying with the natives, we decided any ceremony between those two was good enough for us. They are meant to be with each other."

Looking at George, James continued, "George, I am not here to lecture you or anyone else. A total disregard for the natives is not in your best interest or the best interest of this town. The Chowanoac have been relegated to their 11,000 acres by treaty. Through smallpox and the war in 1877, they have been reduced to but a couple of hundred people. They are no threat to you. Across the river is King Blount and the northern Tuscarora. They can be a threat to this town. The Chowanoac and the Tuscarora are lifelong enemies. But King Blount has seen how they have been reduced and any mistreatment of the Chowanoac or his people could result in another war. Your attitude needs to change if you want to inherit your father's holdings."

James looked to Mr. Hill. "The war took many lives on both sides, as you well remember. Everyone lost friends, family, and property. Treating the Chowanoac fairly will help keep this town from King Blount's introspection. It is good business."

Mr. Hill sat quietly taking it all in. Then he said, "What is it you want?"

Kisis will work for you until her term, which will probably be another seven or eight months. Her wages pay for her room and board and the rest goes towards her debt, correct?"

Mr. Hill nodded, knowing where James was going.

You stipulate in writing what her debt is and what her wages are. During the last month of her term and a month after, I will pay her wages, including the debt portion. That way, if you need additional help in that time, you will be able to hire temporary help until she returns to work.

Mr. Hill said, "What about the child? We will not accommodate an infant in our house."

My wife and I will raise the child until Kisis has paid off her debt," James said.

William added, "We will all help raise that child. They are now family."

George looked at his father and said, "No way. This won't work. The people of this town will hear about this and will not accept it. Your bakery will close when no one buys bread."

Mr. Hill looked at Jonathan and said, "We've applied for another baker to come to town and set up a competition for you. I do not like being blackmailed into decisions."

George blurted, "Look at my face. She did this. How will I be compensated for it?"

Mr. Hill said, "George, stop. We will discuss that issue at another time. Mr. Baker, I listened to and agree with most of what you said.

As long as she continues to work and as long as you pay the debt when she is absent, we can have this arrangement. If either does not happen, you will be responsible and will have to make good on her debt. And, regarding the natives, I did lose friends and family during that war. If every last one of them died tomorrow I would not think twice of it. That is just so you know where I stand on the matter."

George smirked at them all with an evil grin.

James ended by saying, "I'd like all of this in writing if you would. The amount of debt, her wages, her room and food, and what we will be responsible for during her absence. And I'd also like the amount Emilie owes in writing. My brother William here has taken a liking to her, and I know she has never requested her debt amount."

Mr. Hill said, "Why in writing? I have agreed to Kisis, but not Emilie's. She is none of your business."

"Like my brother said, she is now my business," William interjected.

Jonathan said, "Because you are bringing competition here to do your bidding and force us out, your word is only good if it is on paper."

George exploded, "How dare you talk to my father that way."

James faced George as they all got up, about six inches from his face, and leered at him. "Once again, you do her any harm, and you will answer to me. Understood?"

George backed down immediately, the coward he was.

Jonathan finished the meeting by saying, "I'll be in on Friday to pick the written agreements."

With that, they left.

George looked at his father and said, "This is crazy. Who do these people think they are? Who do they think they are dealing with?"

Dexter Hill looked at his son and said, "George, you need to temper your outbursts. Never let others know your thoughts. Be smart. We'll get even with them. Right now, we need the bakery and their services. If and when another baker shows up, we will back and support the new establishment and force the current bakery into bankruptcy. Shut your mouth and bide your time."

As a side note, those we refer to in modern times as Native American Chieftains (or Chiefs) were called Kings in that era, simply because Europeans understood Kings and Kingdoms, which these Native Americans were, Kings of their small realms.

TEN

In 1691, Britain was at war with France during the nine-year war, which took place between 1688 and 1697. In late 1691, the *Coventry* left Virginia and sailed north to Boston, to make a presence. They made some repairs, reprovisioned, and were ordered to the Bahamas. This took about six months in all. In the Bahamas, they received additional orders to cruise the islands as a presence, and then return to England.

In late 1692, Jem saw England for the first time. Although Portsmouth was the only city he visited, he was still in awe of its size, the number of people, and the diversity of the inhabitants. Mr. Beasley had continued to sequester Jem in the head, and he did get the opportunity to go ashore on several occasions.

When he did go on shore into town, he noticed the dress and refinement of the upper-class citizens. They drove in fancy carriages and dressed in flowing and plumed attire, always accompanied by poorly dressed servants. With such refinement, a need for servants or slaves was always necessary for the upper class. He came to realize this was an upper class in any culture, evident in all of his past and subsequent travels. He recalled the telling of how his grandfather went to America from England and what he had to do to satisfy his indentured servitude debt. It was long and arduous.

On one occasion, Jem and Billy were walking near the dock area and passed by an establishment where several ladies were lounging near the door; they were scantily clothed and motioning to them to come and sit. Billy was instantly smitten. But Jem, although aroused, could not bring himself to partake of the women. His thoughts were only of Kisis. It was hard not to relieve himself, but he willed his desires to abate. For now. He gave Billy whatever money he needed to take care of himself. Jem sat on the bench talking to the women while Billy went inside.

He continually thought about Kisis and what she must be going through while working for those people. He prayed for her daily. Would she have changed because of her service? Would George abuse her? What would he do when he returned, if he returned, if Kisis felt differently? He put that out of his mind. He knew they were bound for life, married or not. But what change would happen to her?

The only news they received in Portsmouth was news of the war with France. Nothing from the colonies. The news was usually passed along from sailor to sailor around the water barrel, called the scuttlebutt. The water barrel, called a 'butt' had a hole in it for dipping, called a 'scuttle'. Hence, 'What's the scuttlebutt?' is where that term came from.

In 1693, England was using privateers to support their war effort. The privateers needed able-bodied seamen to supplement their crews. Since they could not conscript seamen as the navy could, they supported their crews through the navy, which would replenish crews through their normal means.

Jem had been a captain of the head for close to two years. Beasley never mentioned him for any other duty. He was ok with it, as long as Beasley left him alone. During that time, the captain and several officers noticed that Jem was always doing his duty. They all wondered why he was never promoted to other jobs on the ship. He was young, very strong, (from raising the buckets of seawater), and very amiable.

In the spring of 1693, several London-based investors assembled a venture known as the Spanish Expedition Shipping. The venture consisted of four warships: *the Seventh Son*, and the frigates *Dover*, *James*, and *Charles II*.

The *Charles II* was commissioned by England's ally, Charles II of Spain, to prey on French vessels in the West Indies. The mission was to sail to the West Indies to conduct trade with other Spanish ships, supply arms, and recover treasure from sunken Spanish Galleons. They were also tasked to capture and plunder French ships as prizes. The investors promised to pay the sailors well and guaranteed a monthly wage much higher than what sailors were making in the Navy.

The time came when the *Coventry* gave up some of their crew. The officers all agreed to send Jem to one of the privateers. He thanked them and they all wished him well.

As fate would have it, some of the officers also wanted to get rid of Mr. Beasley, knowing of his reputation and nickname. He was assigned to the *Charles II* along with Jem. The good news was that Billy, Jem's best friend, was also assigned to the *Charles II*. Nat was assigned to a different ship, and they parted ways.

As bosun, Mr. Beasley immediately assigned Jem to the head. The new crew and officers did not know Mr. Beasley, so Jem started his service on the *Charles II* as a captain of the head.

In the fall of 1693, the *Charles II*, along with the other ships, sailed for Coruña, a port on the Northwest Coast of Spain. The crew received a month's wage but was not paid for the next six months. They were in port the entire time, did not receive wages during that time, and could not leave the ship. They had no money to spend or anywhere to go. Morale was very low.

Keeping the crew busy became harder and harder. The first mate, Henry Avery, tried to keep them busy. On one occasion, Captain Gibson ordered an 'all hands on deck' for an inspection.

First Mate Avery began talking about battle readiness and some training they would do. Billy was in the crow's nest for his watch. As he leaned over to listen, the rail on the small nest gave way and Billy hung precariously on the single floorboard of the nest. Dropping to the deck would be instant death.

Without hesitating, Jem grabbed a coil of rope sitting on the rail amidship and scampered up the rigging of the foremast. It took him about five seconds. He didn't want to climb the top yard of the mainmast since any vibration could loosen the single board of the nest. He quickly tied the rope to the second yard in the middle of the mast (where the cross-piece yard meets the upward mast) and threw the rope to Billy, who was at eye level. Billy grabbed the rope and swung down to the first sail of the foremast, grabbing the rigging. They both descended the rigging together.

The entire crew let out a cheer. The captain asked for Jem to see him on the aft deck near the helm. He and Mr. Avery were there when Jem approached. He touched his cap as a salute and the captain said to stand easy.

"What's your name, sailor?" the captain asked.

"Jem Baker," he responded, somewhat still at attention.

"Mr. Baker," said First Mate Avery. "I have served in the navy, on merchant ships, and on slave ships. I have never seen any crewman climb the rigging and do what you did in the time you did it."

The captain continued. "What is your job on this ship?"

Jem replied, "Captain of the head."

Captain Gibson looked at Avery. He continued. "What was your job on the Coventry?"

"Captain of the head, sir."

"For how long, Mr. Baker?"

Jem replied sheepishly, "Two years, sir."

Gibson looked at Avery and Avery said, "I'll take care of it, sir."

Gibson finished, "Mr. Baker, I commend you for your actions

today. You have done the ship and the crew a good service. As a reward for saving a life, I am giving you this knife and an extra Rum portion for you tonight."

Jem didn't drink. However, he said, "Thank you, sir."

The knife was exquisite. The blade was six inches long and more of a dagger than a knife, pointed and sharpened on both sides. The handle was made of ivory, an ivory that most people did not know existed. It was a tan color, not cream-colored. It had ridges that were highlighted much darker than the main body of the handle, making it look like it had been carved. But it wasn't carved, it was all natural. Jem looked at it in amazement. He let out an audible breath just looking and feeling it. The crew also were amazed at the knife, always wanting Jem to show them the handle.

The captain left and Jem looked to Mr. Avery. "Is that all, sir?"

"No, Mr. Baker. Who was your bosun on the *Coventry*?"

Jem responded, "Mr. Beasley, sir."

Avery became thoughtful. "And he kept you in the head for two years?"

Jem replied, "Yes, sir."

"And, what did you do to make him keep you in the head for two years?"

Jem looked at him for several seconds. "To be honest, sir, which I always am, I did nothing except thwart his advances towards me as a new crewman."

"Ah," said Avery. "Well, tomorrow you report to Lieutenant Myers for sail duty."

Jem's mouth grew into a big smile. "Thank you, sir. Thank you."

Avery continued, "Hold on. There is one condition. If you hear of any issues with Mr. Beasley, you must tell me. I will not have a bosun taking advantage of my crew, in any form. Understood?"

Jem doffed his cap. "Understood. Thank you, sir."

Mr. Avery didn't have to wait long. Jem started his duty as a sailman on the foremast, along with his friend Billy. It was great to be up in the fresh air and not have to work below decks, in the stink of a ship in port for that long. The crew was becoming more and more restless. One night, Mr. Beasley created a stir below deck and was brought before Mr. Avery. The captain was subject to drink. Many times, he was incapacitated, and Mr. Avery assumed his duties.

Mr. Avery read the charges and Beasley was given twenty lashes with the cat. He stared right through Mr. Avery with a scowl and, under his breath heard by the other bosun, vowed to get his revenge. The flogging was witnessed by all hands on deck. Normally, they would be disgruntled with a flogging, as the morale was so low. But Mr. 'Beastly' had it coming, and they were all amused.

Two weeks later, *everything* changed.

ELEVEN

Kisis went through the first months of her pregnancy fulfilling her duties thoroughly and with good cheer. Knowing she was expecting Jem's child made her giddy at times, yet apprehensive at other times. But she had a support network behind her that was just as excited for her as she was. She was always able to go to them.

Mrs. Alston loved Kisis's work ethic and knew she was a great servant to have. Mrs. Hill began to take a liking to her because of her enthusiasm and attention to small details. She conversed with her freely and Kisis enjoyed their conversations. In Kisis's eyes, it was odd how Mrs. Hill was such a nice person and the two Hill men were such monsters. She also noticed how Mrs. Hill was not very close to her husband, who spent most of his time transacting business away from home. He would be gone sometimes for days on trips north, usually leaving George in town to look after town business.

Kisis and Emilie grew closer as Emilie continued with her lessons. One morning, Kisis and Emilie were asked to go to the warehouse and fetch some small items Mrs. Hill needed. From his perch near the bakery, Little Ben saw them approaching the warehouse. Ben was the son of a woman who was owned by the Alsops, another prominent family in town. Their son Henry was one of George Hill's buddies who was part of the altercation in the warehouse. The Alsops owned many slaves from many different backgrounds. Prior to the introduction of African slaves, native people freely traded their enemies to whoever would buy them. Again, it was much more profitable to sell slaves than any other trade they could endeavor. Most slaveholders had a variety of ethnic backgrounds with their slave holdings. The Alsops, Hills, and other families freely made large profits buying and selling slaves. It was big business and the core income of their small empires.

Ben ran down the street to say hello to Kisis, whom he liked very much, and Emilie, who visited the bakery as much as possible to see William. Ben hung around the bakery doing small errands for William for sweets and other treats he would eat or take home to his mother.

The women entered the front of the warehouse and were greeted by a worker whom they knew as a nice man, but that day he had a concerned look on his face. He asked, "Why don't you tell me what you need, and I'll have them delivered this afternoon?"

Kisis said, "It's only a couple of things. It won't take but two minutes."

The man was behind a makeshift counter of sorts. The warehouse spread out behind him through a curtained door. From behind the curtain, the women heard a muffled cry from a female and became alarmed. The man behind the counter gave a very frightened look and said, "Leave, *now!*"

Kisis and Emilie went around the counter and into the front portion of the warehouse. They approached one of the livestock holding pens and saw a young native girl on her stomach, a gag in her mouth, and her skirt and blouse pulled up around her shoulders. Her arms were held down by two men, George looking on while the Alsop son was in the process of getting up after finishing his business. His rear end was bare. Both women gasped. George turned to them and took a step towards them. Just then, little Ben came in, grabbed a nearby pitchfork, and stabbed Alsop in his bare rear end, drawing blood from two different stab wounds. He let out a howl, as George grabbed the boy and forced him to the ground. The other man made a hasty retreat through the back of the warehouse. Henry Alsop was stabbed but not seriously hurt. Both men grabbed the boy and drug him out of the warehouse, as Kisis and Emilie attended to the girl.

She was a Tuscarora, as Kisis immediately knew. She was sobbing in her arms and hugged her tight.

The man from behind the counter said, "Get her out of here before they come back. She belongs to the Alsops."

Kisis and Emilie gathered her up and led her to the bakery, where William wondered what was going on. Elizabeth knew immediately and led the women to her home. The girl was cleaned and rested in her living room.

These incidents happened all of the time. It was common knowledge slaves could be treated however their masters deemed fit. Gang rape was frowned upon. In this case, it couldn't be proven. The women were instructed by Jonathan on what to do and how to act. None of them could act or take reprisals against the Alsops. She was their property to do with what they wanted. Elizabeth would return the girl to them after Kisis and Emilie left. Both girls had to keep quiet and not say a word. Kisis was horrified, angry, and apprehensive. Her main concern was her child, and nothing would endanger that child.

Little Ben did not fare as well. He knew and liked the girl, and when he saw her in distress he acted out of instinct. It was remarkable for a boy of his age. He was whipped by Henry Alsop's foreman as Ben's mother and other slaves looked on. The whipping cut and gashed his back and backside. Being so young with such a brutal punishment, he eventually succumbed to his injuries. Upon his return and finding out about the incident, the elder Alsop was furious with his son for losing an asset that would have paid them handsomely when he grew and could be sold.

The Bakers knew of the Alsop's irritation, and it hurt them immensely to see the callous behavior and attitude toward other humans. From then on, all of the Bakers swore to never own a human being.

Mrs. Alston knew something had happened when the girls returned late. Eventually, word got out of the incident, and she knew the two had been involved. Mrs. Hill also knew something had happened by the demeanor of the girls. She was horrified when she learned of the death of the young slave boy. These incidents happened were common occurrences. Mrs. Hill did not like this at all.

She brought both girls and Mrs. Alston in front of her and instructed them to stay clear of her son and husband. If any issues came about, she was to be told of them. She looked directly at all three and said, "My husband improved our lives through marriage and through my management, not his. I had the royal contacts and the funding for us to begin our lives. It is through my oversight we continue to increase our holdings. I do not like slavery, which is why we only deal with indentured servitude. Everyone answers to someone. Understand this?" She let this sink in for a moment. "Freedom is fleeting. Yet, understanding your limitations and fulfilling basic needs is what counts in the long run. Pure slavery strips a person of their liberty, but more so their hope, which I cannot bear or tolerate." She paused again, thoughtfully. She continued, "My husband has a dark side I have come to know; however frustrating, it is my burden. My son inherited his dark side from his father, not me. But my son also knows I can restrict him, and he answers to me rather than his father. Any issues, you all come directly to me. Understand?"

All three nodded their head and replied, "Yes, ma'am," at the same time.

Kisis was thoroughly impressed by this woman. Knowing her

place as a woman in a man's world, yet it was quite remarkable she was able to impose her influence over her family, business associates, and others. She did it quietly and with grace. Mrs. Hill was not a robust woman, as far as physical activity. She did, however, make her presence known in town with frequent trips, usually accompanied by Emilie. The Hills also socialized frequently with friends and business associates, making their home accessible to many of the townspeople. She was the center of society and would become Kisis's role model from then on, having never had a mother to instruct her in these things. This would prove to Kisis's advantage. Her temper abated using Mrs. Hill as her example, much to everyone else's relief.

TWELVE

Even after the Beasley flogging, the rumblings of the crew and the crews of the other five ships became intolerable. Multiple requests had been sent to London regarding wages and sailing orders. Politics between the English and the Spanish interfered with the intent of the endeavor. Neither was forthcoming after six full months. This led to all five ship captains and crews speaking amongst themselves as to what to do. Captain Gibson stayed in his cabin intoxicated, most days. First Mate Avery, a very capable seaman, was the spokesperson for the *Charles II* with the other ships.

Henry Avery, sometimes referred to as Every, Jack Avery, or Jack Every, was an accomplished sailor and leader. He began his career in the English Navy as a young man, not coming from wealth or social status. By all accounts, he was married and a family man. He furthered himself through service and intelligence, becoming a midshipman on the *HMS Rupert*, a 64-gun warship operating off of the coast of France. The English captured a large convoy of French Merchantmen in 1689 near Brest. He was promoted to master mate and was transferred to the *HMS Albemarle*.

The next action he saw was on the *Albemarle* in the battle of Beachy Head. The English/Dutch squadron was severely defeated by the French and had to give up control of the English Channel. After defeats of this nature, most ships were reorganized, and crews were either traded or outright furloughed. Avery was discharged from the navy in that aftermath in 1691.

Avery then became involved in the Atlantic slave trade, employed by the royal governor of Bermuda to capture and transport West African slaves to the Caribbean and the Americas. He was very good at what he did, ruthless and cunning. He had a reputation among other slave traders for his ability to trick natives into submission.

AT THAT TIME IN HISTORY, THE MOST POPULAR AND MOST profitable commodity traded worldwide was salt. It was the number one commodity throughout time, until the refinement of petroleum in the twentieth century. Salt mines in Asia and Europe were few, located in Poland, Romania, and Germany. These mines were guarded and fought over throughout time. Wars may have had religious context, but the commodity was what was fought over. Countries without salt production had to trade for it. The Chinese were the first to make salt using seawater, a process that is labor intensive and takes time for water to condensate properly and in the right conditions. If trade was limited and salt was not easily accessible, people did whatever they could to get salt.

The same happened with the production of sugar in the 16th century. Sugar cane grew easily in the Americas, and the Portuguese brought the plant to the new world. The drawback to sugar production was the intense labor needed to grow the cane, harvest it, and then produce the sugar. This commodity is what began the slave trade in the new world. Up until that time, captives of wars were kept as slaves by indigenous people, but not to the extent that occurred after a market was established for plantation labor. The trade of sugar boomed. As an example, in the middle of the 18th century, sugar was England's number one import, surpassing salt and all other commodities. The slave trade flourished to accommodate the plantation and sugar industry.

During the last part of the 17th century and into the 18th century, indigenous populations, through war and disease, were decimated. The ability to capture and transport slaves from Africa became much easier and much less expensive to transact. During the next century, over seven million Africans were brought to the new world, most sold in South America and the Caribbean. The colonies mainly used indentured servitude until the production of sugar cane and cotton in the southern colonies became very profitable. Then they began purchasing African slaves in the 1720s. The African slave trade in the United States lasted less than 150 years, a very short time from a historical perspective. The first country to abolish slavery was Great Britain, then France, followed by the United States. This is quite an accomplishment for a country that was less than 100 years old, paying for it in blood and much discord. Issues remained for another century. However, what the United States accomplished was remarkable, again given the historical perspective.

When the opportunity arose to privateer with the English and Spanish against the French, Avery signed on the *Charles II* as first mate.

There were five ships in a squadron that were commissioned by several London investors who assembled this small fleet and commissioned them to raid French shipping. A trade agreement with the Spanish stipulated they sail to the Spanish West Indies and conduct trade, supply the Spanish with arms, and recover treasure from wrecked ships while plundering the French possessions in the area. The investors promised to pay the sailors a guaranteed monthly salary, to be paid every six months throughout the deployment, with the first month's pay paid prior to service. The sailors loved being paid upfront. However, that pay didn't last long.

All five ships knew there was trouble when, in May, during the sixth month of their idleness, the crews did not sail nor were they paid their monthly wages. They could not go off of the ship because there was no money to buy anything in the port. They were stuck on board the entire time. The crews began to look to the officers for supporting a mutiny. First Mate Avery was asked by the *Charles II* crew to be their spokesperson since Captain Gibson was useless. The admiral of the fleet said they were ready to leave. However, the men demanded their pay, which the owners refused to give. Avery went to the other captains but knew they couldn't help.

The crew of *Charles II* voted Avery as Captain, and he invited crews from other ships to join the mutiny. Some forty men agreed and came on board. One was Nat Cummings, Jem's friend from the *Coventry*, who signed on from the *James*, one of the other ships in the squadron. At the all-hands-on-deck meeting to discuss the mutiny, they saw each other and shook hands warmly.

Jem said, "Good to see you, Nat."

Nat replied, "And you, my friend. Is Billy here?"

Jem said, "Yes, and we are both doing well."

Nat inquired, "I have heard rumblings. Beastly was flogged, is that true?"

Jem grinned and whispered, "Aye. And it was a sight. He is still on board, right next to us, and very angry. Watch out for him."

Nat replied, "Aye, I will."

Mr. Avery started, "All Hands. You have voted me captain of this ship. We will depart with the tide. Make all preparations."

From the corner of Jem's eyes, he saw Beasley raise a pistol toward Avery. Beasley said, "You mutinous dog."

In one motion, Jem used his forearm to hit Beasley's arm upward as the pistol fired. At the same time, he pulled his ivory-handled knife out of his waistcoat and stabbed Beasley in the neck, right where he had pointed the sliver of wood two years earlier. Beasley gargled, fell to the deck, and bled out. The crew was stunned. From that time on Jem was a hero. He was the man who dispatched the hated 'Beastly!'

Avery then said, "We will sail with the tide. Any crewman who does not want to be a part of this crew will leave with Captain Gibson when we let him loose."

The other ship's officers saw crewmen rowing to the *Charles II* and then heard the gunshot, and knew the mutiny was afoot. The fortress was alerted. As the *Charles II* left port, they were bombarded by the Spanish in the fort but escaped without damage. Five miles out, Captain Gibson, along with ten other loyal crewmen, were set into a boat and rowed off. The only person he forced to stay about was the ship's surgeon, who was not given the choice to leave. This was customary in that era. A ship's surgeon performed a myriad of duties. Not only was his main job to help keep the crew healthy and tend to the wounded after battle, but he also served as a dentist and a barber.

After Gibson rowed off, Avery sought out Jem. Jem was talking with Nat on deck when the captain approached him. Avery said, "Mr. Baker, I owe you my life, and thank you. That man had it coming, didn't he?"

Jem replied sheepishly, "Aye, sir. But he is the first person I have ever killed, and I'm not sure how to feel."

Avery responded, "In my experience, taking a life is much harder than most people think. To others, it is a way of life who are callous in that regard. Don't ever feel differently."

Jem responded, "Aye, Captain."

Avery then turned to Nat. "You are now on board."

Nat responded, "Aye, sir. Nat Cummings, recently of the *James*. Jem and I served on the *Coventry* together."

Avery said, "That accent. Where are you originally from?"

"Guinea," Nat said smiling.

Avery looked thoughtful and then said, "I may need your services shortly. Stay close to Mr. Baker."

"Aye, sir," Nat ended.

That night, Jem lay on his berth and reviewed how he stabbed and killed Mr. Beasley. He never thought he would ever kill another person. It was instinct and reflex that made him act. He was sure of it. In an odd way, he felt ok, since it was Mr. Beasley. But, deep down, he knew he had crossed a threshold of his life that he would never return from. The knife was now his, no matter what happened to him. It was even more famous than he was.

TWO DAYS LATER, AVERY AGAIN ADDRESSED THE ENTIRE CREW. HE began, "Gentlemen, you have all voted me captain of the ship and I will do my utmost to fulfill your confidence. Not only as a seaman and sailor handling the ship but also as your leader to make decisions as to our endeavors."

Nat looked at Jem. "You understand what he just said?"

Jem grinned and said, "Yes, I do. Don't worry. Most of the crew didn't know what he said."

Avery continued, "We are all now wanted men by the English and the Spanish. I say we are free men, living our lives at our own discretion. We will go wherever we want to and raid whomever we want to."

The crew understood this comment and let out a big "Huzzah."

"We are a small crew, but still need to provision. Then, we make sail for the Indian Ocean, where the Mughal ships are rich and ripe for the picking."

The crew let out another spontaneous "Huzzah."

Later, Jem contemplated the day's events and thought of nothing but Kisis. He would be gone for at least another year, if not more. On that day, it was always difficult to know or receive word from your loved ones. Mail usually took up to a month to cross the seas, longer depending on one's circumstances. He thought of nothing else but returning to her. He dreamt of it and the thought never left his mind. She was always with him.

During the next week, they sailed south from Spain. There was much work to do, to get ready for that long of a voyage, rounding The Cape of Good Hope and its fickle weather. They also rechristened the ship as *The Fancy*, losing the name *Charles II* and any vestige of its prior life. It was now theirs and needed this new name. It was a good ship with three masts; it was fast and sleek, carrying forty-six guns and a crew of eighty. They needed more crew and would soon take care of that issue.

Eighteenth-century pirates were a truly democratic society. They had laws and rules of the sea, voted their officers, and passed judgment quickly on any offenders of those laws, written or plainly acknowledged. Matelotage was an unwritten law that had written discourse between men. An example of one of those unwritten laws was in the event of theft. The theft of items from another pirate was dealt with severely. Taking a fellow pirate's money was one thing. Taking his extra shirt, cap, or breeches usually ended up in a death match. It was just not done.

The decision was made for an equal share of any prize money, with a double share going to the captain.

Upon the death of a fellow crewman by disease or through battle, his belongings were sold to the crew and the captain sent any proceeds or prize share to the dead man's wife or relative, which was stipulated prior to his death. It was a form of insurance they all agreed to and upheld. Captains were expected to oblige, and they did.

At Cape Verde off the northwestern coast of Africa, the crew *of The Fancy* committed their first act of piracy. They raided three English merchantmen of their cargos, which supplied the crew for the time being. Flour, molasses, slated pork, salted fish, and vegetables were a welcome addition to their daily meals. No shots were fired at these three targets. They all capitulated willingly, not wanting to endanger the crews or the ships. Nine additional crewmen were welcomed onto *the Fancy* from these ships. They now had around ninety crewmen.

Then something happened that Jem was completely taken aback by. The *Fancy* sailed to the Guinea coast to purchase slaves from the traders Avery knew from his prior ships. The slaves would be purchased cheaply and sold for a profit on the East Coast of Africa to traders there. Those profits would be used to purchase supplies and other necessities for their continued voyage.

Captain Avery and a dozen men, Jem and Nat included, went ashore and met with a local chieftain. He had a dozen warriors in his entourage with at least thirty captives chained together sitting near the beach. As the chieftain negotiated with Avery, the captives yelled at him in their native tongue. An agreed price was formulated, and the captives were rowed to the *Fancy*. The chieftain and his entourage also came aboard for payment.

Avery approached Jem and Nat on the beach and asked Nat what the captives were yelling. Nat said "Some of these people are from different tribes, probably captured to sell. But some of them are from his own tribe, lower-class farmers and laborers. He is selling them to make more profit for his own people. That is what they are yelling about."

Once all were on board, Avery instructed the bosun and others to arm themselves quietly. Each warrior from the chieftain's party was quietly shadowed by an armed sailor. When Avery gave the word, they were disarmed and put into chains, along with their captives. Avery, being the shrewd slaver he was, had pulled this stunt in the past and was known for it. This chieftain was a novice at the business, and Avery took advantage of it. Selling this lot would be pure profit.

Once again, Jem had a hard time analyzing these events and filtering his thoughts. These were people, people like him and his family, who wanted liberty and the ability to live their lives free from any owner or master. His conscience told him one thing, but the reality was entirely different. He liked Captain Avery and Captain Avery liked him. He held some comfort from this knowledge, but he also knew the shrewdness of the man and would not succumb to his ruthlessness or callousness towards human life.

Once they set sail and after three days at sea, Jem realized the chained slaves had been fed very little and had little to drink. The hold they were held in wreaked of human excrement. He and Nat took buckets of seawater into the hold and splashed their deck of all waste, draining it into the bilge. They then gave them fresh water and boiled rice left over from the previous night's dinner.

Through a grate above the hold, Captain Avery watched Jem and Nat work. When they were done and topside, Avery called Jem over to him. "Mr. Baker," Avery asked.

"Aye, Captain," he responded, knowing what was coming and ready for it.

"Mr. Baker, why are you cleaning and feeding those prisoners? Our supplies are thin to begin with, and giving them anything from our stores puts us in peril."

Jem responded, "May I explain, Captain?"

"Please do," Avery said patiently.

Jem started, "Two reasons. First, those people are our cargo. They are worth much more than the supplies I give them. Diseased and weak upon sale will bring us much less per person, let alone any that may perish during the voyage. Keeping them clean and healthy only works to our advantage. Abusing them costs us in the long run. They will be on board only until we can sell them."

Avery looked at Jem thoughtfully. "You have a sense about you much greater than your age. Mind you, I have traded in slaves much more than you have and have seen more than you have. However, you have a sound point. We will be selling them after we round the cape, in no more than two months' time. Make sure our supplies do not diminish on their behalf."

Jem touched his cap in recognition.

"And your second reason?"

"Sir, my family comes from indentured servitude. I heard my father and grandfather speak of it many times and the loss of freedom and liberty for those in that situation. They also talked about slavery and abhorred it, especially as an institution. Our family will never keep or support slavery in any form. I guess once a person lives it you think differently of it. Seeing those people below in their own waste and hungry and thirsty also brought out feelings I know are not shared by many sailors. Treating them humanely may cause your ire, but it is something I had to do, even if it means giving up my rations."

Jem finished and Avery looked at him for a long minute. Jem didn't know what to expect.

"Mr. Baker," Avery began. "You are a good person. I commend you for wanting to treat those people right. You must look at me and think me a monster. What you don't understand is that slavery has been around since the beginning of time. Every culture, every race of people has been enslaved at one time or another. And, in many different forms. The Egyptians built their pyramids using slaves. The Chinese and Mughals have had slaves for centuries. Chinese concubines have their own caste system. The closer you are to their emperor, the more they are fed and the better they live. The same goes for the harems of the Mughals. People would sell their daughters as concubines knowing they would have a better life as a concubine than as a poor farmer or laborer, even though they would have to physically perform for a variety of owners." He paused and then continued. "Rome had four out of five residents as slaves. Only one in five were citizens. The Praetorium Guard, Caesar's private army, was kept in Rome not to guard Caesar but to keep the slaves from revolting, which they did from time to time. Those slaves also had a hierarchy. The lowest slaves were laborers, oarsmen on ships, and mine workers. The next level was household servants.

Then there were craftsmen, and finally tutors and personal servants. In cities, females are worth more than males. On farms and plantations, males are worth more. The Mongols enslaved many Slavs and Europeans from the cities they conquered. There are blond-haired people in China." He looked at Jem. "Where are you from?"

Jem replied, "Virginia, on the Chowan River."

Avery replied, "I know it well. The Spanish needed laborers for their island plantations: Hispaniola, Bermuda, Antiqua, and others. They buy any slaves that are brought to them. The natives need items the English have: guns, knives, iron pots, blankets, and other items. They quickly learned the value of a slave compared to other trade items. In past wars, captives were kept to replenish the tribe members killed in battle or through old age or disease. They still do that, but some captives, such as men and older boys, are worth much to traders along the coast. They trade in slaves as much as those people down below in our hold."

Jem looked at him thoughtfully and asked, "If I hear you, slavery has always been controlled by a few over the many. Those in power control those who have none."

Avery smiled and replied, "Mr. Baker, those in power and wealth control everything, not only slaves. Look what happened to us. Those in power refused to pay. We were slaves to them for that time period. But we took matters into our own hands. There is a twisted justice to what we are doing. We are robbing those who basically have the power and wealth, those who control many, many lives. And they get rich and even more powerful preying on those whose lives they control. We are called pirates. They are called citizens because they make the laws that favor them and not ordinary people. I would much rather be a pirate and be free to make my own way rather than continue as a slave to those with wealth and power."

"Aye," Jem responded, touching his cap as a salute. Just then four bells rang, and it was Jem's time for watch.

Captain Avery said, "Carry on, Mr. Baker. Keep an eye on our supplies if you would."

"Aye, sir," he responded as the captain walked away.

Jem started his watch with much to think about. His mind, as always, wandered to Kisis. He thought about her situation with the Hills and realized what the captain had been saying. Avery was a smart man, well-versed in the ways of the world. He now had a much different appreciation for him, as ruthless as he was. His ruthlessness would show many times in the coming months.

Thirteen

Kisis was in her eighth month of pregnancy. She never stopped her duties and continued to work and live with the Hills. She and Emilie became very close to Mrs. Hill and they both enjoyed working for her. The environment at the Hill house was pleasant, mainly because George was away much of that time and Dexter Hill spent most of his days at his office.

Events did take a mournful turn when Elizabeth, wife of Jonathan and mother to James and William, passed away in her sleep. She and Jonathan both were well into old age and enjoyed life in her last few years. Kisis felt as though she had lost a grandmother since she was always so kind and informative to her. She helped with her education, not only through books but also through the ways of the English world. Margaret was devastated since Elizabeth was not only her mother-in-law but also her best friend. It was very sad.

Kisis was so impressed when Mrs. Hill attended her funeral. She told Jonathan and William that Elizabeth always had a kind word for her and treated her very well when she shopped at the bakery for sweets. Kisis was also amazed she spoke to Skiko after the funeral. It puzzled Kisis that Mrs. Hill knew Skiko and she had to find out how.

That evening, Jonathan had retired to his room. Skiko was about to leave, but Kisis stopped him. She said, "Grandfather, you talked to Mrs. Hill today. How do you know her?"

Skiko, whose expressions almost never changed, looked down and frowned.

Kisis said, "What is it, Grandfather?" James, Margaret, Jem's sister Katherine, William, and Emilie were all ears and said nothing.

Skiko knew English well enough. But it was very broken. He began, "You remember the girl owned by the Alsops that you and Emilie helped?"

Kisis said, "Yes."

Emilie nodded. "She was a Tuscarora. The Chowanoac were the most powerful people in Eastern North Carolina up until the war. The white settlers kept moving in and taking land. The Chowanoac had close to 800 warriors and decided to stop them. South of the river was Tuscarora land, led by King Blount. They are a different tribe, speak a different language, (Iroquoian versus Algonquin), have different tribes of their own, and have been our enemies since they moved there. We have been here since our ancestors lived here. The Tuscarora have been our enemies for a very long time. The white settlers made a pact with the Tuscarora and made war with the Chowanoac. At the same time, the pox hit all peoples of this region and was devastating to everyone. The Chowanoac were reduced to what we are today after the pox and the war. Many men were sold into slavery in the far south. Your father was one of them, surviving the battles. I watched hidden from a distance as my son Makwa, your father, and other braves were chained and led away. Dexter Hill was in charge of that group of militiamen. Afterward, you already know your mother and grandmother died from the pox. The white settlers gave us our own land, which we now live on and farm, and the Tuscarora agreed to stay south of the river."

He paused and then continued. "Taking slaves was always part of a war. At one point, we raided the city. Many men and women were killed, and we took captives, one being Mrs. Hill's daughter. She was in our village at the height of the fighting. I knew who she was and who she belonged to. Dexter Hill was a fierce fighter. He killed many warriors with his long gun, especially when he looked for his child. When peace happened, he still looked for his daughter and was ruthless. I found his daughter deep in the woods with a family trying to make up for their lost relatives. I knew that peace would not happen as long as Dexter Hill was searching. I took the child and snuck into town, went to their door, and Dexter Hill answered the door with his gun pointing in my face. I had the child in my arms and Mrs. Hill let out a burst of tears grabbing their daughter. He lowered his gun, and I gave the peace sign in sign language. He understood and closed the door in my face. After that, they sent their daughter away to England, I think."

All of them just sat there after his story ended. James finally said, "The Tuscarora are fighting amongst themselves right now, the Northern Tuscarora under King Blount against the Southern Tuscarora, under King Hancock. King Blount and the settlers from here are raiding the southern tribe for slaves. It won't be long before there is another war. I heard that George Hill is taking part in those raids. Slave trading is still very profitable, and the George Hill is part of that business. And that is why he holds no regard for the Tuscarora, which is why they did what they did to that young girl."

Kisis said, "He is such a terrible person."

Emilie agreed by nodding her head.

Kisis continued. "What you did, Grandfather was a very admirable thing. It secured the peace. And, which is why I think Dexter Hill has left me alone these last months."

James responded, "He knows better after we had our little

talk." Looking at Skiko he continued, "Now I know why." Skiko nodded. Kisis started to inquire and Skiko held up his hand, letting her know to leave it alone.

Skiko left with James and Margaret. Katherine stayed with William to take care of her grandfather for the next couple of weeks. Kisis and Emilie left for the Hill's house. Walking back, they couldn't get over what they had heard and were numb from all of the recent events. Kisis knew she was in the last phase of her pregnancy and was starting to feel the effects. Margaret was going to be there in two days to fetch her and take her to the farm, where she would have the baby.

The next morning, after her morning chores, she went into the study, where Mrs. Hill was sitting at her desk writing letters. Mrs. Hill looked at her and said, "I guess you have some questions?"

Kisis looked at her and said, "Not really. Grandfather told us the whole story last night. We are grateful you attended the funeral. I admire you and look up to you, Mrs. Hill. Please understand that. You are someone I would like to become."

Mrs. Hill looked at her and smiled, "Thank you, Kisis. You are whom I would hope my daughter has become. I write to her weekly. My family has taken great care of her, and she is happy, I think."

Kisis said, "It must be hard being separated?"

She responded, "It is, very, very hard. But I know she is safe, being educated, and hopefully, one day will be able to visit when it is much safer here than it is now. I am planning to visit her next month."

Kisis said excitedly, "That is wonderful. I am so happy for you."

Mrs. Hill said, "I am hoping Emilie will come with me, more as a companion rather than a servant. I am hoping she'll agree."

Kisis said, "You need to ask her. I know leaving William will be hard. But it won't be forever."

Mrs. Hill said, "I know those two will eventually get married, and I'm happy for her. I'll only be gone three or four months and we'll be back sooner than you think. I hope she'll go."

Kisis said, "I think she will. She has family in England also."

Emilie did agree to go with Mrs. Hill. William was upset, but he understood. Emilie was going out of loyalty to Mrs. Hill but also was excited to see her family, who lived in Portsmouth, where they would land. She would have a day to visit with them before traveling to London.

Two days later, Margaret came to fetch Kisis and they rode in a wagon back to the farm. Kisis was really starting to feel the strain of the pregnancy, but she did not show any discomfort or complain. She was a Chowanoac and true to her heritage.

A week later, the baby was born at the farm. A baby girl came screaming into the world with a full head of black hair. She had her mother's hair, face, and demeanor. She had her father's eyes and gaze. Margaret was amazed at how Kisis did not complain, struggle, or yell out. As the baby came, Kisis let out a grunt, and she was born.

Holding the new baby, Margaret said, "We need to let the menfolk see their new offspring. Have you thought of a name?"

Kisis looked at Margaret and sheepishly said, "I thought we'd name her Margaret, after her grandmother. We'll call her Maggie."

Margaret cried. "I'm honored."

Kisis said, "We'll name her Margaret Nigamo Baker. Nigamo was my mother's name, which means 'to sing'. And she came out singing."

"Yes, she did," replied Margaret.

Margaret left to get the men. Kisis cried, looking at her daughter, Jem's daughter, and wondered if he would ever get to see his daughter and if she would ever get to know her father. They were worlds apart, but very close in spirit.

Skiko held his great-granddaughter up to the sky and chanted a prayer. It was December 1691, rare that people of that era saw great-grandchildren. Skiko cried tears of joy as he chanted, his white hair blowing in the wind.

They traveled to the village the following week and created such a stir with the baby, they couldn't leave for a long time. Kisis continued to impress her people, and her status rose within the tribe. They doted over the baby and brought many gifts. The tribe was doing well, thanks to Skiko and James, and sweet potatoes.

FOURTEEN

On the sixth day, the *Fancy* was put to sea. Sailing southeast, they encountered a Dutch privateer. Avery was a master sailor. They came about the privateer, who had the twelve guns to the *Fancy's* forty-six guns. From the starboard tack, they let loose a broadside that quickly subdued the smaller privateer. They took aboard ivory, gold, silver, and additional food supplies that were badly needed. Five Dutch crewmen decided to join the *Fancy*.

Two days later, they came upon another Dutch privateer that decided to fight. The *Fancy* gave a broadside to the small ship and boarded her, the crew swinging across the rigging using grappling hooks. Jem was furling the sails with Billy, and they slid down, grabbed cutlasses, and joined the fight. Jem subdued a Dutchman with a slash across his midsection. Captain Avery was on the Dutchman, fighting alongside the men. He climbed onto the bow deck next to the helmsman and captured the helm. Jem and Billy climbed on the bow deck also, and Jem saw a group of Dutchmen with rifles pointing at the captain. He tackled the captain as the volley let loose. A round grazed his chin up to his temple in front of his ear, causing a nasty gash to bleed profusely. The gash went from his lower jaw to his temple, exactly in between his ear and eye. The wound fortunately didn't hit any organs. He also took a pistol round in the shoulder, the ball somewhat spent and laying halfway out of his skin.

Billy came over and put his kerchief on Jem's face. He opened the back of his shirt and squeezed the ball out, giving it to Jem. The captain gave Billy his kerchief to stop the bleeding on Jem's back.

The fighting ceased and the Dutch crew surrendered. Captain Avery took over and they quickly loaded their plunder from the privateer, which consisted of the same ivory, gold, and silver.

They also had many pieces of eight, a chest full, the world's standard currency at that time. A piece of eight was the most common coin used during colonial times. A piece of eight, or Spanish Real, was a Spanish silver dollar divided into eights, or eight bits. Coins were valued by their actual weight in gold or silver, not just on what they looked like. Spanish coins were preferred over other countries' coins because they had a patterned edge which prevented dishonest traders from shaving slivers off of the coins without being detected, an early form of skimming.

Unlike modern times, cutting money was standard. In fact, it was expected that to make monetary change, people literally cut the coins into eight pieces or bits. Something valued at two bits costs a quarter of a Real. That is where the saying 'Shave and a haircut; two bits' originated.

Another four crewmen from the privateer joined the crew of the *Fancy*. They loaded quickly and shoved off of the Dutch ship. Heading southwest again, they encountered another Dutch privateer, probably the third member of this small group of privateers. The *Fancy* once again attacked the slower, less-armed ship, and the Dutch surrendered without a fight. This ship held more food supplies than valuables. It was a welcome addition. Also, another five crewmen from the privateer joined the crew of the *Fancy*. They now numbered close to 150 crewmen, enough to man all guns and maintain the ship as needed.

Jem was aloft as they attacked the last ship. He was woozy and needed to rest from his wounds. As he made his way down the rigging, slower than normal, Captain Avery approached him.

"Mr. Baker," he said. "I once again owe you my life. In time, I will repay that debt."

Jem said, "Sir, I am sure you would have done the same for me."

Avery said, "No matter, I still thank you!"

Billy helped Jem to his berth, smiling the entire way. He said, "Jem, my lad, you have gotten the eye of the captain. Good for you!"

From that time on, any time Avery went ashore or needed crewmen, Jem went along with him, sort of his bodyguard. He completely trusted Jem. The ship's surgeon eventually came to Jem, stitched the gash and the small hole, and pronounced Jem fit for service. He did rest for two days on the captain's order.

The ship sailed to Bioko, a small island off of west equatorial Africa. They careened the ship and spent several weeks working on the hull. Careening is the process of sailing the ship onto a steep beach, which Bioko had several. They then tied the masts to trees on the opposite banks and, using pullies at low tide, forced the boat onto its side. Cargo, ballast, and guns were moved to that side to make the opposite hull exposed. Barnacles, seaweed, worms, and other organisms were scraped from the hull and new tallow, sulfur, and tar were applied to the bottom of the hull. When that application dried, the guns, ballast, and cargo were switched to the other side, and the ship's opposite hull side was then exposed. The process was repeated. This made the ship much faster and more agile with less hull obstruction and drag.

Avery also razed the middle deck, which is altering the superstructure to make it lighter. After removing weight and hull obstructions, the *Fancy* was the fastest ship on the seas. They had a full complement of 150 men and enough guns to attack any ship, even a British Man of War. The crew was cocky and confident. During this lull, Jem was in charge of the slaves. He treated them kindly, and they made no issue. The other crew in their free time went about the island, looking for women and drink, as they always did. Jem had no interest in joining them, always thinking of Kisis and no other.

When they rounded the Cape of Good Hope, it was 1695. Jem had been gone almost five years. He could not believe he was halfway around the world from his home, his family, and his beloved Kisis. The crew was constantly busy, on a ship that battled wind and the sea. Repairs were done daily, as well as cleaning, greasing, and rigging repair. They approached Madagascar, where they sold their slaves, took on some provisions, and headed to the Straits of Aden.

They set sail for the island of Perim to gather additional supplies and wait for a treasure fleet. When going ashore, the inhabitants of the island did not like the English and refused to sell any supplies and did not want them on their island. These were Arab people, part of a society that was closed to outsiders and who thought all outsiders were beneath dignity. Avery bartered with them, asked for fresh water, and they became belligerent. Through interpreters, they basically called the English no better than dogs and they would not lower themselves to do business with them.

Avery laughed to himself, as Jem and Nat looked on. They left the locals and Avery ordered all water barrels to be filled by the crew handling the barrels. The rest of the crew was ordered to burn the entire island of all houses and buildings. He ordered the men to shoot anyone who tried to stop them. Avery went back into the house where the island council was and shot all three of the men himself with his brace of pistols. The entire island was burned to the ground.

They then proceeded south into the Gulf of Aden and met up with five other ships, knowing Thomas Tew of the *Amity* as a worthy privateer and pirate. They joined forces and Avery was elected captain of the fleet since he had the largest and fastest of the six ships. Thomas Tew was the more experienced sailor. However, Avery had the largest ship. Tew had sixty men on the *Amity*, Joseph Faro had sixty men on the *Portsmouth Adventure*, Richard Want had sixty men on the *Dolphin*, William Mayes had forty men on the *Pearl*, and Thomas Wake had thirty men on the *Susanna*. The combined fleet had over 450 men with many cannons.

They lay in wait for the convoy of Mughal ships that numbered over twenty-five. The Mughal fleet slipped past them during the night but was spotted easily in the daylight. The pirate flotilla gave chase. The *Amity* was the closest ship to the fleeing ships and headed straight for the largest of the trailing ships. The pirate fleet was in a V configuration during the chase. The Mughal escort ships, mainly used as fire ships, broke off to attack the trailing ships. As they neared, they were met with cannon fire and ignited immediately, not serving their intended purpose. The other escort ships broke off and sailed and rowed away.

The *Amity* caught the large treasure ship *Fateh Muhammad* and gave it a broadside as it approached. The *Fateh Muhammad* was well cannoned and manned, and fought back. The *Amity* drew close, gave another broadside, and silenced their cannons. The soldiers on the *Fateh Muhammad* swept the deck of the *Amity*, where the crew was crouched behind the rails of the top deck. After the volley, they threw grappling hooks and swung into the Mughal ship, fighting fiercely.

Jem was on the uppermost yard of the foremast. The captain had ordered all sails unfurled. He was on the right yardarm and his friend Billy was on the left. They unfurled the sails and slid down the foremast to attach the topsails to the halyards. As they went back up to the yards, they were able to see the *Amity* attacking the *Fateh Muhammad*. The outgunned *Amity* was taking the worst of the battle, yet it was still fighting the bigger ship and causing extensive damage. The *Amity* crew was boarding the *Fateh Muhammad*.

The *Fancy* was coming around at full sail to broadside the *Fateh Muhammad's* stern. Jem had a bird's eye view of the battle from his perch on the foremast yard. The captain had ordered this top crew to stay put so that as soon as they pulled alongside for a broadside, the sails were to be furled back to stop any movement of the *Fancy*. As the *Amity* pulled alongside the *Fateh Muhammad*, the *Fancy* came around and gave the *Fateh Muhammad* a broadside to the stern as the guns bared. Captain Avery then rammed the stern of the *Fateh Muhammad* and ordered sails furled up. The ship stopped and swung around like a lever, and with grappling hooks, the *Fancy* was able to pull alongside backward to the *Fateh Mohammed* on the starboard side, opposite the *Amity* on the port side. At that point, the battle ceased, with the *Fateh Muhammad* boarded on two sides by two different crews. Although the Mughal ship had more soldiers and sailors, the pirates were more ruthless, subjugating the crew within minutes.

Once the sails were secured, Jem and Billy almost flew down the rigging and grabbed cutlasses stowed near the bow for their use. They joined the battle, swinging onto the Mughal ship. By the time they arrived on the deck, the fighting was over.

All hands searched the ship for treasure and Jem witnessed first-hand the brutality of men seeking treasure. They quickly tortured the captain and several officers to find the location on the ship with the cargo they sought. Jem could not believe what he was watching. Such rampaging and crazed brutality.

The slave rowers from below deck, probably forty in all, were brought to the main deck and inspected. Jem was amazed at the different looks and races of the slaves. There were, what he guessed Chinese or Japanese, blond Northmen, Europeans of all kinds, black Africans, and some islanders. The Mughals enslaved many of the people that came from every walk of life. Jem had seen slavery firsthand, including his own, and did not like any part of it.

Only ten to twelve of the slaves were considered healthy and were given cutlasses and knives. In a few moments, they were slashing at their Mughal masters with abandon, killing them and throwing them overboard, inflicting the pain and brutality they had suffered at their hands.

Jem looked to the *Amity* and saw Captain Tew lying dead in a pile of his own intestines, his abdomen eviscerated by a cannonball. He approached Captain Avery, standing on the stern forecastle of the *Fateh Muhammad*, and motioned down to Captain Tew, lying on the severely damaged Amity. Captain Avery took charge of both ships.

They found the treasure hidden on the *Fateh Muhammad*, which was vast. Gold and silver bars, gold coins, spices, textiles made of silk and cotton, and stores of grain and other merchandise. The *Fateh Muhammad* was a prize. Once the *Amity* was repaired to sailing status, both ships would head to Madagascar for further repairs and the sale of the prize ship.

Captain Avery knew the *Ganj-i-Sawai* was the larger ship and had more treasure. Since the *Amity* was severely damaged and without a captain, he ordered all of the treasure quickly stowed on the *Fancy*, kept only thirty crew and the slaves on the *Amity*, and took the rest of her remaining crew onto the *Fancy* to chase and capture the *Ganj-i-Sawai*.

Two of the four other four ships of the flotilla caught up with the *Fancy* and they went after the *Ganj-i-Sawai*. The *Dolphin* had been badly burned by the Mughal escort ship that caught fire and rammed them. Most of its crew went onto the *Fancy*. The *Suzanna* had rudder issues and stayed with the *Amity* to all escort the *Fateh Muhammad* to Madagascar, where all ships would be repaired.

The chase lasted for almost six days. The Mughal ship was large and well-armed. Yet, it was very sluggish in open and rough water. The *Fancy* caught up to her first, as the *Portsmouth Adventure* and *Pearl* lagged behind.

The *Ganj-i-Sawai* was an opponent to be feared. It had eighty guns and a contingent of 400 musket-bearing soldiers on board, as well as over 600 passengers. Aiming a broadside in waters that had six-foot swells was very hard. The cannon had to be fired during an upswell, or the balls would fall harmlessly below the water line of any opponent. The Mughal ship fired first as the *Fancy* came around its starboard side. They were not practiced gunners, as the broadside fell harmlessly into the sea under the Fancy. The English gunners were well-practiced and experienced at their tasks. The first broadside from the *Fancy*, on the upswell raked the deck and three lucky shots hit the mainmast a quarter of the way up the mast. It collapsed onto the deck and into the sea, virtually stopping the ship. As the *Fancy* came around for another broadside, a cannon on the lower deck of the *Ganj-i-Sawai* exploded and started a huge fire amidship. Their crew rushed to put the fire out as the *Fancy* gave a second broadside. At that close range, the soldiers on the Mughal ship sent a volley into the *Fancy*, killing and wounding many of the *Fancy's* crew. However, the smoke and fire were out of control and the soldiers had to help extinguish it. The crew of the *Fancy* swung over and climbed aboard the *Ganj-i-Sawai*. The *Pearl* pulled up alongside, the crew clambered aboard, and a battle took place that lasted two hours, with terrible hand-to-hand fighting. The ship finally surrendered.

The captain of the *Ganj-i-Sawai* was in his cabin and armed his ten concubines as the pirates broke into the room. Several tried to fight but were no match for the men. They were quickly subdued, as two were killed outright.

Jem had once again been in the foremast with Billy as the *Fancy* came around for the second broadside. As the grappling hooks were deployed, they furled the sheets, scampered down the rigging, and swung over to the Mughal ship. They joined the battle.

Jem was facing some of the soldiers who had muskets with

bayonets. He stabbed two men and was then slashed across his back by a third, who swung his musket instead of stabbing. The slash was superficial, and Jem was able to deal with the soldier, killing him with a quick stab. He and Billy stayed together, moving about the deck with the other crewmen. They did not go below decks, since the crewmen that had preceded their arrival were dealing with those decks. They stayed topside and captured surrendering soldiers and sailors.

Jem watched the brutality with fear and fascination. The battle put him in a trance, a state of rage. He became an animal, as most men do. He didn't want to kill. Was it survival or just following orders? He knew he had to fight to stay alive, which is all he wanted to do. After this battle, he knew he might have to fight again. But he promised himself that if he did survive and somehow got home, he would never fight again unless he was forced to. At least now he knew how to fight. These were all conflicting thoughts.

If Jem was conflicted in consciousness about the battle, what he was about to witness was much, much worse.

The decks of both ships were littered with dead and dying men. Blood flowed in small streams over the gunnels and into the water. When it was finally tallied, the *Fancy* had lost close to eighty men killed and twenty seriously wounded. Over half of their men were out of action. The *Pearl* had lost one-third of their crew, and the *Dolphin* limped to the scene a day later.

The *Ganj-i-Sawai* had lost sixty sailors, 250 soldiers, and ten of the slaves rowing on the third deck, along with two concubines. Most were killed from the explosion and the subsequent fire on that deck. None of the 600 passengers were killed during the battle. The captain watched as sailors and soldiers were tortured to relinquish the hiding places of the treasure. The captain was brought up and also tortured. Then something remarkable happened.

The passengers were all lined up on deck to witness the

torturing so they would understand to give up all of their coin, jewelry, refined clothing, and anything else of value they had. In the midst of this crowd, it suddenly parted, they bowed their heads, and a young woman walked through them. Jem figured she was royalty and they all were scared of her. She approached one of the mates and demanded that they all be released, in the name of the Mughal. She had two bodyguards with her along with three ladies-in-waiting, Jem guessed.

Captain Avery, standing on the Fancy's stern deck, motioned to one of the mates and another seaman who accompanied him. They dispatched the bodyguards with pistols, shoved the ladies-in-waiting to the deck, and proceeded to strip and rape the royal lady in front of the crowd. A general gasp went through the crowd, and it became incensed as other seaman surrounded them with pistols and sabers. The high and mighty men were killed as they stepped forward to stop the rape. Their women were then dragged into different corners of the ship. The rest of the men eventually were tortured. A general raping of the passengers ensued and lasted for two days. Some of the female passengers actually slit their own throats and fell overboard, not wanting to be abused as the others were. Others were tortured to extract and relinquish the treasures hidden on the ship.

Jem was sickened by the rape of the royal lady. Then he became thoughtful. Here was a young woman whose family was the most powerful family on that continent. She was raised privileged, but in the open seas, she was powerless and the victim of circumstances beyond her control. Jem realized power and wealth did not always protect a person. Whoever had the power at that time, controlled others.

He and Nat both swung back to the *Fancy*. He approached Captain Avery, who still had his hackles up from the battle. Jem knew not to spar with him. He requested he and Nat help with the transfer of items from the *Ganj-i-Sawai* to the *Fancy*. Avery agreed and put him in charge of stowing supplies and treasure coming from that ship. He trusted Jem to report accurately what was taken and stowed.

After three days of loading treasure into the hold, Avery was ready to depart. He only had seventy men on his ship, and between the *Dolphin* and the *Pearl,* he had another forty men. All of the treasure was put aboard the *Fancy* and the captains agreed to meet later to split the loot. The *Ganj-i-Sawai* was cut loose and sent on its way after the captain was able to muster enough men to sail the ship.

Fifteen

pon returning to the Hills after giving birth, she continued her duties as if nothing had ever happened. Mrs. Hill and Emilie left for England, hopefully, to be gone only for several months.

Kisis had become much closer to Mrs. Hill. In the first week of her return, she approached Mrs. Hill and had a long conversation about Skiko and Mrs. Hill's daughter. Mrs. Hill had always thought Skiko was a good man who wanted to do the best for his people. She never forgot the kindness he had shown them. She would reveal much more at a later date.

Before Mrs. Hill left for England, they brought in another young lady to help Mrs. Alston. She was Tuscarora. She spoke Iroquoian and knew very little English. Kisis was Algonquin and understood very little of that language. But through universal sign language and some small words, they were able to communicate.

Her name was Ikar, which means moon in Tuscarora Iroquoian. They all decided to call her Moon. She was young, probably in her late teens, and somewhat malnourished. Mrs. Alston took care of feeding her and couldn't believe how much she ate.

She stayed in Kisis's room so Kisis could start tutoring her to learn English. Each night, as with Emilie, Moon began to pick up more and more words, especially words that would help Mrs. Alston communicate her needs.

Moon had come from the southern Tuscaroras. The territory that would eventually become North Carolina was split in two by the Tuscarora. The northern band occupied the area from the Chowan River west toward the mountains, and south to where present-day New Bern is along the Neuse River. The southern Tuscarora was led by King Hancock, from the Neuse River south to the present-day South Carolina border, but they resided mainly along the Cape Fear River. The land was empty and fertile hunting grounds. Both King Blount and King Hancock wanted to rule all of the Tuscarora. King Blount allied himself with the white settlers during the Chowanoac War and continued aiding them, dealing with King Hancock. King Hancock did not want anything to do with the English and wanted to live and respect the old ways.

King Blount was promised aid by the English settlers and received guns, which were prized possessions. He helped the English sell captives when they raided the southern band. George Hill was a major player in this business, taking the place of his father who was the master at slave trading. Mrs. Hill was aware of that side of their total business ventures. She did not like it but did not stop them. Dexter had seen atrocities during the war, and it scarred him for life. He loathed all natives.

Moon was a slave, bought and paid for by George, and he treated her terribly. In the months Mrs. Hill was gone, several incidents erupted that could have turned out worse than they did. Moon was scrubbing the hallway floor as George walked by. His boots were splashed by the water she was using on the floor. He scowled down at her while she was on her hands and knees, and cursing her, he kicked her in the side saying, "Watch what you are doing, you stupid bitch."

Both Kisis and Mrs. Alston heard Moon grunt and heard

George's remark. They both ran into opposite ends of the hallway at the same time. George turned to Mrs. Alston and said, "You need to train this stupid bitch better. She just threw dirty water on my clean boots."

Mrs. Alston apologized as George turned and saw Kisis staring at him. George blurted, "You have something to say?"

Kisis just stared at him, her jaw moving slightly with her fists clenched. She stared a hole right through him. He turned and walked out.

On another occasion, George had come home late one evening very drunk and was yelling as he came up to the front of the house. Mrs. Alston roused both girls and told them to go out to the stable, find the stable man, and hide until George passed out. They stayed out there for over an hour until Mrs. Alston gave the ok. They heard and saw George roaming around upstairs looking for Moon, and maybe Kisis for that matter. They all knew how mean he was sober. There was no telling what could happen when he was drunk.

Dexter Hill pretty much left them alone, and George was gone for two months at a time on slaving raids in the south, making the house very quiet. They went about their chores, and on several occasions, Dexter was invited to a friend's house for Sunday dinner. Kisis was able to leave earlier to visit Maggy. James and Margaret, and sometimes Skiko, would be at Jonathan's house. Katherine always made a large Sunday meal, and it was great family time. Kisis always brought Moon and even Mrs. Alston on several occasions.

Kisis loved the time she spent with Maggy. During those five or six hours, Kisis would not let Maggy out of her sight, even holding her while she slept. Margaret sometimes cried, knowing the pain of being separated from her child. But Kisis persevered, knowing in several years it would be over.

Mrs. Hill and Emilie returned after spending over eight months in England. The visit with her daughter was exceptional and she didn't want to return. Her daughter had no ambition to go back to the colony given the circumstances of her departure. The colony was still wild and nowhere near as civilized as London. She would stay in London and take care of her mother's holdings there.

Emilie had become very close to Mrs. Hill and she could not understand how she dealt with her overbearing husband and ruthless son. Divorce was uncommon during that era, and she persevered as well as she could. She understood Emilie and her desire to marry William. They came up with a plan to pay a modified amount for her to be released from her servitude. Mrs. Hill would make sure Dexter would agree to it.

In 1692 William and Emilie were married. It was a large wedding and many of the townspeople attended. William was a solid member of the community and was well-respected by all. Marrying Emilie, who was also known by many people, was somewhat of a scandal, given her standing as an indentured servant, but it was overlooked as all knew they were very much in love and had spent all their free time together.

The Baker family was growing. Katherine was the caretaker of Jonathan, who was not doing well. James and William spent as much time as they could with him, as his health was failing fast.

Katherine also was being courted by several of the young men in the town, whom James and William kept a close eye on, as well as they could.

The years went by quickly. Maggy was now four years old and was a beautiful child. She had long black hair that was kept tied into a single braid in the back. Her eyes were amber, a combination of her mother's black eyes and her father's light brown eyes. Her face and determination were all her mother. She was primarily raised by Margaret and James, yet still spent much time with Kisis. She was smart, outgoing, and amiable like her father, and every day she reminded them all of Jem. They all missed him terribly. Kisis's intuition told her he was still alive, but she didn't know if and when he would ever return.

Jonathan had passed away in 1694, and Katherine had married

and moved to another house in the town. William and Emilie kept the original house Jonathan and Elizabeth had built when they opened the bakery. It was still the Sunday gathering place for the family, and Emilie and Katherine both still worked at the bakery. The family stayed close.

Sixteen

As the *Fancy* prepared to depart the *Ganj-i-Sawai*, the slaves from that ship requested to see the captain. Avery had Jem bring the leaders aboard the *Fancy* to see what they wanted. There were close to 100 of the rowing slaves on the ship, and they did not want to go back on the ship as their station would not change with the Mughals. Instead, they asked to be shipped to Madagascar to either join other crews or find their own way to their homelands.

Avery agreed. The Mughal ship would have to sail home without the services of their rowing slaves. All of the slaves on that ship were released, close to 250 total. One hundred fifty went on board the *Fancy* and the other 100 were split between the *Dolphin* and the *Pearl*.

Jem was amazed that 600 passengers had 150 servants. They were all slaves, and they were all different in race and culture. Everywhere Jem went slavery teemed. Out of 1000 people on that Mughal ship, 25% of the people were slaves. How did this happen? How did they keep those people? From the beginning of time, why did man think he could keep another man against his will? Then he thought of the princess and her fate. She would return home violated by the same men she and her people enslaved. Poetic justice or just the law of nature, the strong violating the weak. Where was the freedom and liberty that all men wanted?

Jem again promised himself he would never keep another human nor be kept by another human.

The captains of the three ships met and decided the *Fancy* would keep the treasure and they would all sail together and meet on the northern tip of Madagascar to divide shares. That night, while the crews of the *Dolphin* and *Pearl* were still on the *Ganj-i-Sawai* having their way with the women passengers, the *Fancy* slipped away and ran southwest for the open sea and Madagascar. They arrived on the southern tip of Madagascar a week later. Captain Avery had made the deal with the slave rowers and part of it was for them to help load the Fancy with fresh water and other provisions prior to them being released. They provisioned in record time as the rowers wanted to be free. By the time the *Dolphin* and *Pearl*, as well as the other ships, reached Madagascar, Avery and the *Fancy* were long gone.

Avery knew he could not use the Mughal coins anywhere else in the world and not be found. So, they purchased eighty African slaves in Madagascar as liquid currency to be sold elsewhere for pieces of eight.

The total treasure from both ships was estimated at £200,000 to £600,000. That meant the eighty remaining crewmen of the *Fancy* would all see over £2000 each. Or 3000 pieces of eight each, depending on where they traded their gold, silver, and gems. The average wage for a skilled laborer in 1700 was approximately 100 pieces of eight a year. If a piece of eight equaled a pound in those years, Jem now had a lifetime of salary from that one haul. They all did.

Jem decided to cash all of his gems, gold, silver, and other loots, such as silk, in for pieces of eight. He did this in Madagascar and with the other crewmen, who wanted to keep the gold and silver. He lost some during the transaction, but he still ended up with 3800 pieces of eight, as that currency was still predominant in the colonies. They filled two small chests full, and they were very heavy. Jem kept the coins near his berth and was sure they would not be bothered. It was the code, and they all had plenty.

Jem, Nat, and Billy went ashore on Madagascar the night before they departed. All three had plenty of silver to have a good time. They talked Jem into accompanying them to a tavern that also served as a brothel. Jem was tempted several times but could not bring himself to be with another woman other than Kisis. His commitment to her was that strong. Billy and Nat partook, of course, and they rode Jem for the next couple of weeks, describing their experience. Jem just laughed and took it in stride. They knew his connection to Kisis could not be broken.

The ship departed and stopped on Ascension Island where they caught sea turtles, enough to feed them the rest of the way to the Bahamas. Some of the foreign crewmen that didn't want to go to the Bahamas stayed on Ascension Island, to wait for the next ship that passed by. They hoped they could purchase transportation aboard. After that stop, the *Fancy* headed for the Bahamas. The slaves were now used to help sail the ship. They didn't mind the work, since it was better than being chained in the hold.

Once again, Jem and Captain Avery talked during one of Jem's watches. The captain came onto the stern deck where Jem was talking to the helmsman. Jem said, "Good evening, Captain."

Avery said, "Aye, Mr. Baker. I tried to read but it didn't help me sleep."

Jem said, "I have more books that I bought in Madagascar. How they made their way there I have no idea. Has to be from passing ships. You are welcome to them if you need different reading."

Avery said, "Aye, that would be grand. You are the only

crewman who reads. I find that startling because, at one time, we had over four hundred men on this ship."

Jem said, "Right now, one of the men from the *Suzanna* who came aboard before the *Ganj-i-Sawai* is a Tuscarora from my part of the world. His language is Iroquoian and the language of my wife is Algonquin. We are teaching each other words and phrases. It's something to do to pass the time."

Avery said, "You are something, Mr. Baker."

Jem continued, "There is a book I tried to read by William Shakespeare. I'm having difficulty reading and understanding it."

Avery laughed and said, "As do most people. You have to read it and re-read it several times to understand what he is saying."

Jem responded, "Then why did he write it that way?"

Avery said, "William Shakespeare not only wrote several ways, but he invented a new way to speak. Yes, it is hard to understand. Educated people have a hard time understanding him. But what he did was to raise the consciousness of language to a point where it is eloquent to use speech to correctly convey a point rather than use colloquialism and slang, which leaves a guttural and false sense of idea conveyance. For example, the men on this ship curse, use foul language, and cannot convey an idea, let alone formulate one."

They both chuckled at that remark.

Avery continued, "There are several reasons people curse and use filthy language. One, they are uneducated, and that language is a substitute for proper language. Why? It gives them a sense of power. That language is confrontational, and it dissolves any conscientious effort from the receiving party to communicate further. Like I said, it's guttural and most people won't lower themselves to that standard. Another reason is people are raised hearing that language and think it is the way all people talk. If they become educated, then they realize how informal and terrible it really sounds. And lastly, some people want to ingratiate themselves with others by using that language as a common bond.

'If you don't curse you can't be one of us' mentality. That mentality also goes beyond cursing, with the use of dress, clothing, and other aspects of that group."

Jem said, "I don't quite understand that last comment."

Avery finished, "You know the language of your wife. Does that make you a native? No. But it does ingratiate you with those people since you are able to communicate and are not a complete outsider. Look at the slaves we have on the ship now. They are close-knit since some have the same language and most have the same customs, even though they are from different tribes. There is a bond there and it segregates them from others unless they learn to come out of that seclusion."

Jem responded, "I know what you mean now. Kisis's people are trying to assimilate with the English so as not to perish. They may lose their identity, but they will survive."

Avery became thoughtful and then said, "Well, it's about time to sleep. You have made me think too much tonight, Mr. Baker. Tomorrow, please bring me whatever books you have, and I'll give you what I have that you haven't read."

"Aye, sir," Jem responded. "Thank you, sir."

The *Ganj-i-Sawai* finally made its way back to the harbor in Surat, damaged and barely seaworthy. The news of the attack spread quickly. It was the abuses of the pilgrims that inflamed the people, a sacrilegious act that, like the raping of the women, was considered an unforgivable violation of their Muslim religion. The local Indian governor immediately arrested the executives of the local EIC, who were English subjects and held them as ransom. Aurangzeb quickly closed four of the EIC's factories in India and imprisoned the officers.

Emperor Aurangzeb was livid. The loss of his treasure ship and the defilement of his relative had serious consequences for the English of the East India Company. Avery's attack threatened the trade agreement the East India Company had with the Mughals. They were to protect all shipping in the Indian Ocean as part of that agreement. That meant the trade they had with England was in jeopardy. Not only did the East India Company (EIC) build and support Men-Of-War, but England also sent Men-Of-War into the Indian Ocean. That trade agreement had to be protected for England to maintain its sea dominance, in that ocean and other oceans.

The EIC promised to pay all financial reparations and agreed to police the ocean from that time on. They also had Parliament issue a bounty and reward for Avery and his crew. In 1696, Avery was the most wanted man in the world, and news eventually spread to all corners of the known and traveled world at that time. It was the first worldwide manhunt in history. The crews of the other five ships that participated in the raid were also livid that Avery did not split the spoils with them. They also attempted to head to the Caribbean, on the chance they would catch him there. The *Fancy* was a much faster ship and the other ships had repair issues to deal with before they could round the cape and head west.

Once the *Fancy* reached the Bahamas, Avery bribed the governor to let them stay. When word of the manhunt reached the governor, he had Avery brought to him and they discussed what to do. In return for his passage elsewhere, Avery once again bribed the governor by giving him the *Fancy*. The governor immediately renamed the ship and changed its outward appearance so no one would be the wiser. The slaves they had bought in Madagascar were being held in a seaside warehouse awaiting sale.

The Bahamas have a history that is not well known. The entire population of all of the islands was decimated by the slave trade that took the indigenous people and sent them to the mines in Cuba. From the time of Columbus to the late 17th century, the islands were basically void of any industry or people for that matter. Escaped slaves and others tilled some of the soil on farms that were left by previous owners. But the farms were subsistent and not commercial.

The English saw the potential of the land and founded Nassau in 1670. They built a fort named Fort Charles and started settling that island. The intention was to establish plantations on the islands surrounding Fort Charles.

There were frequent wars with the Spanish and Fort Charles was used as a base for English and other privateers against the Spanish. The fort and the entire town were attacked and burned in 1684 by the Spanish. It was rebuilt in 1695 and renamed Nassau.

Avery and the whole crew of the *Fancy* were pleasantly surprised in 1696 when they arrived and saw the town growing and thriving. Avery had known the problems it had and wanted to use it as a low-key base where he could get supplies and do repairs. The activity of the port was incredible, with many ships anchored offshore and many ships coming and going.

Since 1670, the plantations on the other islands were still working and growing. Cotton, sugar cane, and rum were being produced in good amounts, even though the town had burned and only been rebuilt the prior year. Nassau was the hub for supplies and products coming and going.

From an English merchantman, the news came to the governor regarding the price on Avery's head, and that of the crew of the *Fancy*. The governor had already been bribed for the *Fancy* to stay. However, the governor also knew British naval ships would soon arrive. Something had to be done. He called Avery in and that is how they came up with the plan to sell the *Fancy* and change everything about it so as not to draw attention to it. Once it was changed, the governor quickly sold it to a merchantman, prior to any naval ships arriving.

Jem was on land again and knew he was closer to home than he had been in the last five years. He kept his loot on board until the last minute of the *Fancy*'s sale. Then he, Nat, and Billy rented rooms at an inn near the port. Billy had been severely wounded across his forehead during the battle with the *Ganj-i-Sawai* and was recuperating nicely. They walked around Nassau during the day and spent most evenings in the taverns. None of them were big drinkers. But they did like to talk to other sailors about the adventures they had. The three never once said where they were from or what ship they were on. They only talked about their time in the British Navy.

During the day, Jem spent much time at the pier and liked walking through the open market, buying fruit, vegetables, and meat that wasn't salted pork or salted fish. There were many different peoples in Nassau, coming from all parts of the known world. It truly was a melting pot of races, ethnicities, and cultures. Jem loved it. He also watched the women working the stalls and constantly ached for Kisis. He felt her presence everywhere and couldn't shake the yearning. Down deep, he knew she was ok, but he still missed her terribly.

He needed to find and speak to a merchantman that was going to the Carolinas. At that point in time, there were none. So, he knew he would have to stay at the inn until one would come along. Knowing he would negotiate passage, he purchased clothing that included new breeches, a new shirt, and a long coat similar to what ship captains wore. Finally, he bought a tricorn hat of good quality. His long hair and hat somewhat hid the scar on his face.

A week after their arrival, Jem was walking the market and he saw two indigenous men pulling a cart of supplies through the street. The man on the left handle slipped and stumbled and the man on the right admonished him, saying, "Get up, you fool" in Chowanoke Algonquin. Jem couldn't believe his ears. Did he hear right?

The man who stumbled looked up at his partner and said, "Shut up," in Chowanoac. Jem followed them to the wharf and saw them loading a small skiff. In English, Jem asked them where they were going. The man who admonished his friend was definitely in charge of the two. He responded in broken English that they were going to the next island over, which was Paradise Island. Jem asked the two Englishmen in the boat if he could visit the plantation on Paradise Island, and they agreed. There were about six other indigenous men in the boat, along with two Englishmen.

The island had one large plantation on it. They produced rum from the sugar cane they grew and were doing ok, but not well, given the appearance of the house and surroundings. Jem introduced himself to the owner, Mr. Galway, and told him he was looking around, contemplating whether he would stay to invest his efforts or leave the islands. Mr. Galway, in his past life, was a privateer and understood Jem immediately. They became friendly and Jem was given a tour of the plantation. Jem let it slip that he had been fortunate and may want to invest. He spent the day and that night on that island. They were going back into Nassau the next day. He would hitch a ride back.

That evening, Jem told the owner he wanted to take a stroll. By himself, he made his way to the slave quarters. The huts the slaves lived in were very crude and mostly open to the elements. The group he sought saw him coming and quickly became quiet and alert. There were about twenty people gathered around a firepit, including men, women, and children. There was another group of slaves around a different fire. They were mainly of African origin.

Jem approached the fire and looked at their apprehensive faces. He asked them, "Who is your leader?"

They all looked at him and said nothing.

Then, in Chowanoac he asked, "I mean you no harm. Who is your leader?"

A man on the far side came up to him face to face and said, "How do you know our language?"

Jem looked at him very closely.

Makwa had grown up during the height of the Chowanoac power and prestige in Eastern Carolina. He knew the peaceful and plentiful times. He was about five feet six inches tall, had black hair, now cut very short, and had deep black eyes. His jaw was pronounced, and his nose was large and regal looking. His body was wiry, given their substandard diet. But his stance and bearing were still strong. He was the image of Skiko and Jem saw Kisis in the man's face and demeanor. The man's jaw moved slightly back and forth, looking at Jem ominously. He knew that Skiko's son was not killed in the war but was taken prisoner and sold into slavery, along with many of their people.

The war between the Chowanoac and the settlers of eastern Carolina ended in 1677. The tribe had been decimated by disease and by several battles with the white settlers and their Tuscarora allies. Makwa and twenty braves were the last holdouts. They had been cornered in a makeshift fort of felled trees and logs and were surrounded by over thirty English militia and over fifty Tuscarora warriors. The Chowanoac had some women and children with them inside the enclosure. The muskets were too hard to fight against and the English offered them surrender and capture rather than a fight to the death. Makwa was not a chief, but he was able to convince the leaders to surrender and live rather than die right there.

They surrendered and were immediately put into chains. The Tuscarora sold them to the Yamasee further south who in turn sold them to the Spanish in present-day Florida. They then were sold to different plantations throughout the Caribbean.

Skiko had watched from a distance with two other warriors and knew they could do nothing to help them, but he knew Makwa was alive and hoped he would someday be able to return.

Jem studied the slave for a quick moment.

The Chowanoac repeated, "How do you know our language?"

Jem looked him straight in the eye and said, "You are Makwa, son of Skiko, father of Kisis." He paused and continued. "My wife!"

Makwa's jaw dropped. He was stunned. The entire group was stunned. They all looked at Jem, as Jem stood there smiling. It lasted a good two minutes. Then they all jumped up and started asking questions all at once, at the same time. Makwa held his hand up for silence, but it did not help. They wanted to know about family, relatives, how he married a Chowanoac and other questions.

Jem sat down and spoke for the rest of the evening, as they all gathered around and respectively listened. He told the story of how he and his father met Skiko and Kisis when he was six years old. He told of his mother teaching Kisis to speak English and how she educated them both, being a teacher. He told them of the pitiful state of the Chowanoac and how his father James and Skiko planted together and farmed the land. He let them all know the Chowanoac were doing fine and living better than they had in years past. He told them where the village was and how he spent time learning their language and their ways.

After speaking for over three hours, he finally ended with his marriage to Kisis and the circumstances of their separation, and how he had spent five years at sea. His goal was to get back to her as soon as possible. Questions were posed and he answered them as he spoke about family, friends, and who was left in the tribe.

It was late and they all began to leave to get what little sleep they could. Jem stayed with Makwa, and they devised a plan. He told Makwa he had enough money to buy them and that they could then buy passage back to the Carolinas. Makwa couldn't believe what he was hearing and said he would support anything Jem wanted to do. Jem asked Makwa, "How many of you are there?"

Makwa answered, "We were many when taken by the English. We were all sent here to different places. Upon arrival, many were sent elsewhere. We were bought and sold several times before coming here. We've been here for at least eight years (counting the years as well as he could). Now, we have eight men from our tribe, four of whom are married. They have a total of six children. That would be eighteen people in all."

Jem did some quick math. If he were to buy the slaves Avery had brought with him and traded them to the owner for the eighteen Chowanoac, then he would be able to purchase them outright. He told Makwa, "You make sure they all keep quiet about this. No one is to talk to anyone else. Keep them quiet for now. I'll be back in two days."

The next morning, Jem approached the owner of the small plantation and asked him several questions. He first asked him about the natives other than the African slaves. The owner said he was ok with the men. But they had wives and children, more mouths to feed than he could afford. His plan was to sell the women and children since the men were much more valuable working the fields than the women. A couple of the women worked in the main house. So, he would not want to sell them, since they did the housework.

Jem said, "Mr. Galway, I would like to buy the natives, all of them, including their women and children. I have access to recent imports of slaves and would like to trade them. If I made you a good deal, would you be willing to negotiate?"

Mr. Galway said "Son, everything has a price. What are your terms? I would like thirty pieces of eight for the men, twenty pieces of eight for the women, and ten for the children."

Jem said, "That comes to 380 pieces for the lot."

Mr. Galway said, "That's correct. And, I'll take ten pieces each for those two female Melungeons. They are almost worthless."

Jem asked, "Melungeons?"

Mr. Galway replied, "Melungeons come from your part of the colonies. The French named them since they are so different. Mixed breeding of Africans and Europeans the Spanish termed Mullato. Mixed Natives with Europeans are called half-breeds. Then there are mixed Europeans, Natives, and Africans. The French termed them Melungeons, which translated means 'mixed' or 'mingle,' They started using that phrase about ten years ago. If you look at them, they look African but have blue or green eyes. And some even have blond hair with African features. Others look native with sharp features, and no facial hair, yet they have blue eyes and auburn, or even some red hair. Those colonies are definitely a diverse lot of people."

The Melungeons are a unique story in the history of North America. They were a mixed race of Europeans, Africans, and Native Americans. Given the era of slavery and the era of discrimination of any people who were not 'pure,' the Melungeons created a class of people not accepted by any culture or society that deemed them different. Or more precisely, inferior to pure classes of people. This, of course in today's standards, is not acceptable. But in that time and era, it was logical and accepted by all people. After the Tuscarora War of 1711 to 1713, the remaining Tuscarora fled north to the Iroquoian Federation of Tribes. The Melungeons were not able to follow the tribe. They were not accepted by the native tribes nor by the Europeans. They would not be accepted north or were not able to stay and be accepted by the European colonists. This was a large group of people living together due to their circumstances being different. They eventually migrated to western Virginia, eastern Tennessee, southern West Virginia, and eastern Kentucky, all in the mountainous regions of Appalachia. Their descendants still live in these regions today, given the remoteness of the region and the mountainous terrain. That class of people no longer exists, given the melting pot that America is. Their descendants are no different from anyone else in any other region of the country.

Jem answered, "Wow. Ok, I'll take the Melungeons also. That will be 400 pieces in total. I'll be back in two days." They shook, and he left in the skiff, smiling at Makwa the whole way.

When he got back to Nassau, he found Captain Avery at a tavern and Inn. They met in the tavern. He began, "Captain, the slaves you have in the warehouse. Are they still there?"

Avery looked at him quizzically. "Yes, Mr. Baker, they are? And look at you! You seem to want to captain a ship the way you are dressed."

Jem laughed and asked, "Have they been sold?" Avery looked at him again with a wary eye. "Mr. Baker, knowing you and your aversion to slavery, why do you ask?"

Jem went into the entire story with the captain. Avery was amazed that the odds of finding these people here, especially the father of his wife and son of his adopted grandfather, were extraordinary. It took him two mugs of ale to digest the tale. Jem let him know exactly where they were going and described the Chowan River once again for Avery, who finally asked, "How will you get them home?"

"Passage would not be hard for this little number of passengers. Anyone with a small ketch could take us. It would be a matter of finding such a ship."

Lifting his eyebrows, Avery said, "There are plenty of ships here already. You will not have trouble finding passage, for the right price."

Jem smiled and said, "I think I may be able to take care of that." They both chuckled.

Avery said, "Mr. Baker, keep a low profile. Do not spread that money around. The world is looking for me and anyone who was with me. Now, for each slave, I'd want thirty pieces of eight, unless you buy all thirty. For all, I'd take twenty-five pieces, 750 total."Jem negotiated and they agreed to 650 pieces of eight total.

The next day, Jem hired three skiffs and they were all transported to Paradise Island, where Mr. Galway was waiting for them, as he saw them coming toward the island. They sat under a tree while they negotiated. Mr. Galway offered Jem twenty pieces of eight for all thirty. Jem said he paid thirty pieces for each, the owner being a hard bargainer. So, Jem said, "You are basically looking for twelve pieces of eight average for the natives. You give me the natives outright and I'll give you the Africans for fifteen pieces of eight each. That would be right around the original twenty pieces each."

Mr. Galway did the quick math, and they struck a bargain. For an additional twelve slaves, he would reap many benefits from them as opposed to the women and children. The transaction had cost Jem 220 pieces of eight. But it was better than costing him

400 pieces of eight. He was satisfied with the deal, as was Mr. Galway. The Chowanoac gathered their belongings quickly and loaded into the skiff a couple of hours later. Jem had arranged to keep them in the same warehouse the Africans were kept.

The next morning, through a contact of the governor via Captain Avery, Jem negotiated with a ketch captain to transport them all to Carolina. They boarded the two-masted ship and Makwa chanted a prayer for the voyage they were undertaking. They were all still in shock and disbelief they were going home. Nat had spoken to Jem the night before and had told a story of how he was in an altercation with some men and was almost knocked unconscious and kidnapped, for sale as a slave. Billy came to his rescue and fought off the scoundrels. Nat knew he had to leave and asked Jem if he could go with him. Jem agreed and asked Billy, who was standing on the wharf if he wanted to join them. Billy wanted to get back to England in the worst way, so he declined. They all three hugged each other and swore their brotherhood to one another, a bond that is lifelong.

The boat left the quay as Jem and Nat waved goodbye to their friend, whom they thought they'd never see again.

SEVENTEEN

The trip to North Carolina usually took anywhere from three weeks to a month. The ketch entered the gulf stream, and the weather was good. They made the trip in less than three weeks, Jem and Nat helping the small crew with the sails and whip staff helm. Jem loved being the navigator, as the whip staff was on the after deck and not hidden in the companionway since there was only one deck. He watched the compass and took direction from the captain and manned the helm for as much time as he was allowed.

Makwa and everyone moved about the boat freely, sometimes getting sick over the side. It was a terrible feeling, and everyone helped each other. They sailed into the Pamlico Sound through the Ocracoke inlet, the captain knowing the shoals there, and expertly sailed north. He took the helm from that point on and entered the Albemarle Sound. Jem had negotiated with him to sail the boat past the Town on Queen Anne's Creek and go as far up the Chowan River as the boat could. The boat had a shallow draft. But anchoring and getting everyone ashore would take time since their skiff was small. They ended up going ashore about two miles south of where Jem had originally met Kisis, and he knew he was only several miles from his home and only several miles from Skiko and the village.

Jem asked Nat to run ahead to the village and ask for Skiko. As Nat entered the village, he was met with skepticism. They asked him what he wanted, and he asked for Skiko. Skiko was in his abode and it took several minutes for him to get up and he had to be helped outside. The two neighbor ladies propped him up as he came outside. He was the only elder left of the original council. His hair was long, white, and his face showed his age and health.

Nat said, "I come from far away. I was told to tell you Nunnaumon (your grandson) has returned bearing gifts."

Just then, an uproar was heard at the gates of the village. The men entered the gates of the stockade and people rushed to them, recognizing relatives, other family, and friends. Skiko looked at Nat, who had a big smile on his face. The crowd parted and Makwa approached his father. Skiko gasped, stood up straight on his legs, shooing the women off, and held his son's face in his hands. Tears streamed down both men's faces as they looked into each other's eyes. Finally, Makwa said, "My father, I have returned. You can be at peace."

Skiko said, "I prayed to the spirit for this day for many years. It has come to pass. My son, Makwa, the bear. My son has the fortitude of a bear and has never quit."

Then Jem approached them in his tricorn hat and long coat. He approached Skiko, taking off his hat he said, "Numohshomus. I have returned bearing gifts."

Skiko hugged his grandson and looked at them both. "My grandson has been gone a long time. It is good to see you are well," as he moved Jem's head to look at his scar. "You have seen much and have traveled far. Have you seen Kisis?"

Jem said, "No, not yet. She will be surprised."

Skiko looked at him and said, "Yes, she will. As will your daughter, Maggy!"

Jem was stunned and couldn't speak. Finally, he said, "How? When?"

Skiko said, "She was born right after you were taken. She is five years old now."

Makwa looked at Jem and said, "I have a granddaughter as old as when I last saw my own daughter. This truly is the work of the spirit."

The entire village brought out food and drink and offered it to the returned family. There was much singing and laughter. The celebration lasted for two days. The wives and children of the returned men were all accepted graciously and without bias. The Chowanoac were truly the first people to be put on a reservation and the first people to accept all others, regardless of ethnicity. The Melungeons were accepted as well, even though they mainly spoke Iroquoian, with some English and some Spanish. Stories and tales of travel and events and occurrences in all of their lives were told and absorbed by everyone, a true oral history.

Makwa asked Skiko about the elders that were no longer with them. Skiko told him the events that occurred after they were taken and sold into slavery, after the last war. He also told him the story of Jem and Kisis and their relationship with the Bakers. He told Makwa that James and Margaret were great people and that they should be honored on all occasions. They saved our people.

After several hours Jem quietly excused himself from the festivities and told Skiko he had to find Kisis. Skiko looked at Makwa and said, "Go with your son and meet your daughter and granddaughter."

Makwa and Jem both smiled at the statement, and they were off. Jem couldn't carry the two heavy chests of coins. They were small but very heavy. He hid them behind Skiko's wigwam, along with his weapons and Nat's stash. He let Skiko know what was in them. When Skiko saw the coins, his eyes went wide. He looked at Jem and said, "Be careful, grandson."

Jem looked at him and said, "I understand and I will be careful."

Jem and Makwa approached the farm several hours later and didn't recognize it. There was a small group of wigwams at the far end of the woods, as they approached the tilled and planted fields. Those wigwams were for the workers who stayed there during the planting and harvesting seasons. Jem could not believe the amount of planted earth his father had extended since he had been gone. There were probably over one hundred acres of sweet potatoes, growing well.

The house and barn looked the same. As they approached the house, several workers stopped and gathered to see the strangers. Makwa knew none of them except a young man in his twenties whom he knew was the son of one of the returned men. He greeted him and told him to go see his father who had returned. The man dropped his hoe and ran off into the woods, followed by a couple of others. James saw the commotion from the barn and walked out to them. Jem saw him coming and took off his hat. James let out a whoop that startled and scared Margaret, who came out onto the porch. She recognized her son immediately and came running. As they all hugged, she cried, kissing and hugging him for what seemed minutes. They finally gathered themselves and Jem introduced Makwa and told them he was the son of Skiko and Kisis's father. Margaret looked at him and saw Skiko and Kisis, immediately. She told him of their looks and how Kisis looked just like him. She asked them in, but Jem said he had to see his wife and daughter. Margaret understood and James asked another one of the workers to hitch up the buggy for them to ride into town.

On the way, Margaret talked constantly. She mainly talked about Maggy and how she stayed at the farm most of the time, as Kisis was still working for the Hills. At one point, Jem looked at his father and said, "That won't last very much longer. Later I'll tell you the whole story, beginning to end."

James had an idea of what he meant. They couldn't talk during the ride since Margaret talked the whole way. She let him know his grandparents had both passed away, William married and was running the bakery, and Katherine had married, but was still working at the bakery. Jem tried to take it all in, as Margaret caught him up on all of the news. She also told him of Kisis's relationship with Mrs. Hill and that George was a monster and was slaving in the south with the Tuscarora King Blount. Makwa got a stern look on his face and James saw it. James looked to Makwa and said, "We need to talk about the Tuscarora. We have an uneasy peace with them, given what they did to you and your people. For now, they are leaving us all alone." Makwa just nodded his agreement.

When they arrived at the bakery, Jem went in first, as James and Margaret stayed by the buggy. He was greeted by Emilie, who had no idea who he was. He asked her, "Is the proprietor in? I have a complaint."

She looked at him quizzically, stared for a couple of seconds, and said, "I will get him. Please wait here." She went into the oven room where William was finishing up Sunday work. She said, "William, there is a pirate outside who said he has a complaint."

William dusted the flour from his apron and walked out into the commercial area. Five feet from the counter he saw Jem and leaped over the counter and tackled him to the floor. Emilie gasped and saw they were both laughing, hugging, and crying at the same time. Once their composure was regained, William turned to Emilie, and before he could say anything she asked, "Jem?"

Now Jem was confused. William laughed and said, "Jem, meet Emilie, my wife. She and Kisis are best friends."

Jem looked at her, looked at William, and then said, "I am happy for you both." Then Katherine came busting in and hugged her brother.

Emilie said, "I looked into your eyes and saw Maggy immediately. It took me back."

Jem said, "Where is she?"

Katherine said, "I just saw her in the market with Kisis. They are buying vegetables for dinner. It is Sunday and we always have Sunday dinner."

James, Margaret, and Makwa walked in, and introductions were made. They were all astounded that Kisis's husband and father were both there.

As Jem left the bakery, Emilie gave him a piece of candy that Maggy loved and that Kisis sometimes gave her. He walked down the street to find his wife and daughter. Everyone else stayed behind to let the three reconnect in their own way.

Maggy let go of her mother's hand as Kisis was looking at tomatoes to feel for their ripeness. The tomato barrow was set up close to a tavern that had benches along its outside walls. Kisis felt the absence of Maggy and turned around. Maggy was talking to a man sitting on a bench holding a piece of candy: a man who was sunburned, had long hair, a scruffy beard, and looked like a pirate. His head was down, and his hat covered his face. Maggy was not scared and talked to him like anyone else. Kisis hated the fact that Maggy had her personality and backed down to no one or no situation. Kisis walked quickly over to her, grabbed her hand without looking at the stranger, and pulled her away saying, "Maggy, please leave this gentleman alone." She turned her back and she walked away quickly.

Jem quickly stood up, took off his hat, and said, "Kiki!"

Kisis froze. She turned, dropped the basket of vegetables, dropped Maggy's hand, recognized Jem, and flew into his arms, wrapping her feet around his waist. She began kissing him all over his head and face, crying and talking half English and half Chowanoac. It sounded like gibberish between her kisses. She stopped abruptly, looking at the huge scar in front of his ear that ran down to his cheek. "Oh, my god. Oh my god. What happened to you?"

Just then Maggy came up to her mother pulling on her skirts. She was scared of what she was seeing. Both Kisis and Jem knelt down to her height. Kisis said, "Maggy, this is your father." She looked at him and held up the piece of candy.

Jem said, "Yes, it's yours. You can have it."

She looked at him closely and touched the scar on his face. "Did that hurt?" she asked.

Jem answered, "Yes, it did, very much." He looked at Kisis and said, "She is definitely your daughter!"

Kisis slapped him on the shoulder and they both laughed. Kisis said, "Yes, she has my demeanor. But she has your kindness and your eyes. Look at her. Isn't she beautiful?" They all three hugged and held each other.

Jem picked her up as she opened the candy. Kisis gathered her vegetables and walked back to the bakery. Kisis looked at Jem and said, "My, but look at you. You have twice the bulk you had when you left. How did it happen?"

Jem said, "I have much to tell. Five years is a long time and many things happened. I've been to the other side of the world and back. Much to tell and I plan on telling you all of it."

They walked together teasing each other as though they had never been separated. As they approached the bakery, Jem got serious, stopped walking, and said, "Kisis. There is something else. I know seeing me has been a shock. But I have another shock for you."

She looked at him quizzically. They continued walking and as they approached the bakery, Makwa walked out. Kisis froze, looking at him as though he was Skiko years earlier. His hair was short and had streaks of gray. But he was almost a clone of her grandfather. Thoughts raced through her mind for almost half a minute and memories came flooding back from her early childhood. Her legs buckled when she realized who she was looking at. Makwa reached for her and steadied her. She said, "Noosh (father)."

He smiled widely. They hugged tentatively and she looked at Jem.

Jem nodded and said, "I know."

She then looked at her father and said, "Grandfather?"

Makwa said, "He made us come look for you!"

Makwa looked at his granddaughter and asked, "Can I have some candy?"

Maggy pointed to the bakery and said, "In there."

Makwa took her from Jem and walked with her hand in hand to the bakery.

After Kisis gathered herself, they walked into the bakery where everyone was waiting. It was pandemonium for at least ten minutes. That Sunday dinner was the most memorable they ever had and would be talked about for years to come. It lasted well into the early hours of the morning.

Jem walked Kisis back to the Hill's house. She woke Mrs. Alston, who came down to the back door in her nightrobe and was introduced to Jem. She was embarrassed, being in her night clothes and all, and she told Kisis to go back with him and to be there in the morning. Kisis was very grateful, thanked her, and said she'd be there bright and early on time.

They walked back together and spent the night in each other's arms, with Maggy between them of course. He looked at her right before they fell asleep and said, "I dreamt of holding you for five years, every day, every night. Never did I dream of holding two of you!"

EIGHTEEN

William, who had an internal clock, woke everyone the next morning before dawn. They all dressed quickly because Kisis had to be at the Hill's house to start her day. She usually took breakfast to Mrs. Hill and didn't want to be late. Maggy stayed with Margaret at William's house and James went back to the farm. He would be back later to pick them up and to find out the results of the reintroduction of Jem to the Hills. It would be an eventful day, to say the least.

On the way to the Hill's house, Jem kept a tight hold on Kisis. He kept nudging her and she kept pushing him away, knowing what they both wanted. She kept telling him she didn't want to be late. He told her he would meet her later and they would sneak off for him to ravish her and she would give him a proper homecoming. They laughed and giggled the whole way.

Mrs. Alston was dressed and greeted them at the kitchen door. She saw Jem, and smiling, she told him to go home, clean up, and come back later to meet Mrs. Hill. She looked at Kisis and said, "Later, you'll need to go to the market," winking at her.

Kisis smiled and thanked her. She said, "Maggy would not leave us alone last night."

Mrs. Alston looked at Jem, "Bring Maggy along later. Mrs. Hill loves her. Right now, you look and smell like the sea! Come back after you have cleaned up." They all laughed.

Jem went back to William's house, took a bath, and changed into clean clothing. His nice overcoat was sent to a neighbor who would wash and clean it to look just like new. The clothes he had purchased in the Bahamas were of much better quality than the clothes he wore on the ship, as an ordinary seaman. Most of the crew wore white britches, which extended halfway down the calf, a loose white or chambray shirt, and usually a small beret-type 'duck' cap to keep the sun off of their heads. Contrary to popular myth, 17th-century sailors wore shoes called ditcher boots. It was almost impossible to work on a ship barefooted. The salt from seawater and the heat of the wooden decks would make feet swell and they would get very tender. Certain tasks required going barefoot, like washing the decks. The abrasion of the rope rigging, and the wooden yards made barefoot work temporary while furling and mending the sails. Jem threw away most of his crewman clothes except for his ditchers. They were well-worn and of high quality. He could wear them on land as well as at sea. However, he did purchase a nice pair of shoes pertinent to everyday wear.

Maggy did not leave him alone, except when he shooed her away before getting into the bathtub. She was back and watched him shave and finish getting dressed. She talked non-stop. Jem was amazed at how smart she was, like her mother. At almost six, she was reading and doing arithmetic well above her years. Margaret loved teaching and loved Maggy as a student, like her mother.

They walked hand in hand to Mrs. Hill's house. Jem had to answer all of the questions she had about being at sea, where his scars came from and why he left, etc. He was patient and loved answering every question she had. He didn't want to patronize her with silly answers. She was too smart for that. But he did tease her a little, just to avoid some of the harder questions he couldn't and didn't want to answer. It was banter they'd have the rest of their lives.

They went into the kitchen of the house and Mrs. Alston said Mrs. Hill sat in the parlor. As they entered the parlor, Maggy ran to a rising Mrs. Hill, she curtseyed and gave her a big hug. Mrs. Hill smiled from ear to ear and asked, "And how are you today, dear Maggy?"

Maggy said, "Just fine, thank you. This is my dad!"

Mrs. Hill turned to Jem and extended her hand. "Very pleased to meet you, Mr. Baker."

Jem said, "Please, call me Jem. There are too many Mr. Bakers in this town." They both laughed.

Mrs. Hill looked at Maggy and said, "I think Mrs. Alston has some fresh biscuits in the kitchen, right out of the oven. Would you like to have one?"

Maggy said, "Oooh. Yes, ma'am." She looked at Jem, and he shooed her away.

She offered Jem a seat and they sat opposite each other around a small tea table, Jem in a chair and Mrs. Hill on a small couch. A young lady came in with a tray of tea. Mrs. Hill asked, "Would you like some tea, Jem?"

He said yes and the tea was served by a Tuscarora in a dress that was somewhat large on her. She finished and Mrs. Hill thanked her. As she turned, Jem looked up and in the Tuscarora dialect said, "Thank You. You are very kind!"

The young girl stared at him for a second and smiled broadly. She then caught herself, lowered her eyes, and left the room. Mrs. Hill looked surprised. She said, "That young lady has been here for over three weeks and that is the first time I saw her smile. What did you say? You know her language?"

Jem replied, "I thanked her. Hearing her own tongue took her back and she lost herself, but only for a moment. I take it she has been very hesitant working here?"

Mrs. Hill said, "Jem, I don't like the situation we are in here. We have many businesses in this town, one of which my husband has been in for years, which I have never liked. Indenture is one thing. Outright slavery is another issue entirely, one which I do not like but have to deal with. My husband has not partaken in that industry for a long time. However, my son is a different matter, and I can no longer control him. This young lady, Ingrid, was brought to us by my son. I have taken it upon myself to make sure she is treated fairly and becomes somewhat educated. Just so you know, we have had servants come and go. Your Kisis has taught them to read and write on her own time and to educate them in ways they would never have the opportunity. I love Kisis and will miss her dearly. I am assuming, the reason for your visit?"

Jem smiled and said, "So you know, you have made her life here not only tolerable, but she has come to love you and enjoys your company immensely. For that, my family and I are forever grateful. That is the reason I have come to visit you today, to thank you, and to ask your blessing to complete the indenture contract with your husband. Kisis is very emotional regarding this situation."

Mrs. Hill replied, "We have become very close. I am sure we will continue as friends going forward. You most certainly have my blessing." She then lowered her voice in somewhat of a conspiratorial manner and said, "Don't worry about my husband. He has already been told what to do." They both smiled and sipped their tea.

Just then, there were loud voices in the hallway. They heard George say, "What is this half-breed doing here again. Mrs. Alston, I told you not to let her run around here when I'm home." They then heard Kisis say "Maggie, come here now!"

George walked into the parlor and began, "Mother, why is…?" He trailed off when he saw Jem stand up. The blood in his face drained, but he gathered his composure quickly, looked at Jem, and said, "The criminal has returned. Nice scar!"

Mrs. Hill got up and exclaimed, "George!"

Jem's stare went right through George, who for the first time, was intimidated. His body language showed it, and Jem picked up on it. He turned to Mrs. Hill and said, "Thank you for the tea and the visit. You are too kind. I will see myself out, with Maggy." He turned and left.

Jem went into the kitchen and looked at Kisis and Mrs. Alston and smiled. "We'll be leaving now," he said very calmly. Mrs. Alston took Maggy by the hand as they all went outside. Kisis stopped Jem and said, "I can't leave just yet."

Jem looked at her quizzically and said, "Why not?"

Kisis looked into his eyes and quietly said, "The girl, Ingrid. George brought her here about three weeks ago. He has been raping her probably twice a week. Mrs. Hill doesn't know about it. If either of us (pointing to Mrs. Alston several feet away) say anything to her, George will fly into a rage and take it out on all of us. He is a monster."

Jem looked at her sternly. "Has he ever touched you?"

She said "No, never. He knows better. Your father and Skiko threatened him thoroughly."

Jem smiled. "Let me see what I can do with Dexter Hill today. I'll let you know. I'll take Maggy home for now."

Kisis kissed and hugged him and said, "Thank you!"

As Jem stepped outside, Ingrid came around the house and motioned to him. In Iroquoian, she said, "My father is a nephew to King Blount. He does not know I was taken by this man he does business with. There are twenty others kept in the warehouse by the water. Some are from our band. If King Blount finds out there will be trouble."

Jem had a hard time understanding her, but he eventually understood what she said. He motioned it was ok, and she left quickly.

Kisis asked, "What is it, Jem?"

He said "There are twenty more Tuscarora held in their

warehouse by the water. I'm not sure what I can do. But I'll mention it to Dexter Hill in our meeting."

That afternoon, Jem met with Dexter Hill at his office. He was cordial enough and they got down to business. Jem asked for Kisis's release, and Jem gave him the small amount that was owed. Dexter also mentioned to Jem that Mrs. Hill had taken a liking to her, and if he would, please do not keep Kisis from seeing his wife.

Jem said, "Mr. Hill, I have seen firsthand the relationship between Mrs. Hill, Kisis, and Maggy. I would never come between that."

Dexter Hill thanked him, and they exchanged the money and the paperwork involved.

As they were finishing, George Hill came in and stopped short when he saw Jem. He snarled at his father, "What is going on, Father?"

Dexter Hill looked at George and said, "Mr. Baker has just paid the remainder of Kisis's servitude. She is now free from her services to us."

George looked at Jem and sneered, "Good riddance, and that little half-breed, too!"

Jem stared at him and calmly said, "That little half-breed is my daughter. I do not take kindly to your insults."

George responded back, "I really don't care what you think, you criminal."

Jem contemplated his response as Mr. Hill said, "George, that is enough!"

Jem finally said, "George, you and I both know the circumstances of that day the fire started. I will not go over it again. But, true to your nature, you now have some twenty Tuscarora held in your warehouse, one of which you are consistently raping. Most people turn a blind eye to what others do with their slaves. But through my travels, I have seen slaves of all types, including concubines, Africans in chains, and rowers on ships that are chained to their oars. I have seen what they do to their masters when they are released, and it is not a pleasant sight. Some of those natives you are holding are from King Blount's clan of the Northern Tuscarora. If he were to find out you are arbitrarily taking his people, there will be repercussions that will not only involve you, but everyone in this town and surrounding area."

Dexter Hill jumped up and scowled at George, "Is this true, George? Are you holding Blount's people?" George looked at Jem and said, "You are a liar. I don't know where you got that information, but you are a liar, you criminal!"

Jem responded, "We'll, I think I'll visit King Blount and see what he says about it. Makwa is back and he and Skiko want to assure King Blount that they want to live in peace. This could help their cause."

George flew off in a rage and vehemently cursed Jem. He said, "I'll get even with you, mark my words." He stormed out of the office.

Dexter Hill looked at Jem and said, "Is this true?"

Jem looked at him and said, "The girl Ingrid in your house. She is a grandniece of King Blount. She gave me that information today. And your son is abusing her. There could be trouble."

Dexter Hill looked at Jem and said, "Just so you know, I have been trying to get George out of that business for a long time. I did it in my youth and was good at it. My wife has made me see differently, and we agreed to stop George. But he is headstrong and cannot be swayed. I think he has angered the wrong people and will bring us all misfortune."

Jem looked at him and said, "I don't think my involvement will help. But if you need me, I will help. In my travels, I have seen much and do not like the industry and what it does to people. I feel for that girl and her people being held. I'll do whatever, on your advice only."

Dexter Hill thanked him, and Jem left.

Nineteen

Jem walked to the bakery, thinking about the conversation he had just had. He knew George Hill would be out to get him. He had to warn Kisis and the whole family. George was a dangerous person.

He went into the bakery and Kisis was there with Maggy, Makwa, and Margaret, talking to William and Emilie. Kisis looked up at Jem and said, "Father has come to get us. Grandfather is very sick and asking for us all to visit.

Jem looked at everyone and said, "I'll hitch up the wagon. We all need to go now."

They drove to the farm and picked up James. When they reached the village, the people were all somber and the women were crying. They went into Skiko's wigwam, and he was being attended to by several women. They propped him up and left the family alone. Maggy went to Skiko and sat in his lap, as she always did. He hugged her and looked at everyone. Kisis began to cry. He looked at her and said, "Granddaughter, do not cry. I have asked my family here because my time is short." He coughed. He looked at them all and said, "There has been much change in my life, more change than I would ever have expected as a young man.

I leave you all these parting words. Change will happen. Embrace it." He looked at Makwa. "My son. Forget your past. Do not seek vengeance for what happened to you. Look to the future and make it what you want." He then looked at James and Margaret. "You have been family to us all. I leave knowing our family is in good hands. I thank you for your friendship and guidance these last years. And, for help making my granddaughter who she is." He looked at Jem. "Your riches do not lie hidden here. Your riches are all around you. Keep that in mind as you move to the future. I have food, water, shelter, tobacco, a good fire, and people around me who care for me, as I cared for them in their times of need. This is what is important; the simple things in life we take for granted."

James looked at Jem. Jem just nodded to Skiko and then to his father.

Then Skiko looked at Kisis. "My Granddaughter. The light of my life. You have brought me happiness that knows no bounds." He squeezed Maggy and she let out a giggle. "You have always been in my heart, and I will be in yours for the rest of your life. Look to me for strength in your times of need. I will be there." He stroked her cheek. Kisis could not hold back her tears. She wept openly. Margaret tried to comfort her, weeping herself.

Skiko bid them all farewell, and they left as he lay back down to sleep. Makwa said he was staying with his father.

James went to Jem and asked him what Skiko was talking about. Jem asked his father to pull the wagon to the back of Skiko's wigwam. He did, and he helped Jem with the two chests of silver and Nat's two chests hidden under furs and some brush. When they were placed on the back of the wagon Jem opened one to show his father. James's jaw dropped open and Jem said, "You don't want to know."

James asked, "What are you going to do with this?"

Jem said, "We need to hide it in the barn for now. Do you have a safe hiding place for it?"

James said, "I do. A place your mother doesn't even know

about. I hide some whisky there from time to time. It's under the floorboards in the back stall that goes underground about two feet. If the barn burns, the hole will not."

Jem said, "Perfect."

James said, "You have to tell me about this."

Jem responded, "I will. It is a very long story, one that Kisis wants to know too."

They returned to the farm and the ladies went in to make dinner. James and Jem hid the silver in the barn and they both thought it a good place. They also agreed to tell Margaret and Kisis where it was, just in case something ever happened to them. James re-hid his whisky in another stall.

That night, after dinner and after Maggy had gone to sleep, Jem told everyone his tale. It took almost three hours to relay all of the details with very little interruption or questions. Kisis now understood how his chest had become so bulky. They all understood where the silver came from, and they were all appalled at his telling of the battles he was in and the men he had killed. He explained the scars on his back. His mother made him take his shirt off to see. Nat also told stories about his scars, especially the one on his arm. They both laughed while telling about the incident where Billy was cut across his forehead, which was really superficial but bled for two days. All Billy was worried about was what the scar would look like.

One of the biggest revelations to them all was the stories they told about slavery and the taking of humans into bondage. They could not believe that concubines actually were sold to better their lives. It was somewhat confusing. They were appalled by what Captain Avery did to the chieftain who sold his own people for profit. Was it justice? The stories of the rowers chained to their oars and how they massacred their masters once set free were eye-opening. It was all too much for them to comprehend in one evening. Jem knew he would get more questions as time went on.

Jem's and Kisis's old rooms at the farm were now taken by Nat and a couple of other workers. Jem and Kisis would sleep with Maggie. Jem looked at his mother and said, "Kisis and I are going for a swim at our water hole. Please do not wait up for us." Margaret laughed and James just shook his head. He went to the storage area and came out with a couple of blankets.

He said, "Maggy will be just fine."

Jem and Kisis never made it into the water. Their desire was such that they hardly made it to the shoreline before they were naked and rolling around in the grass. It had been a long time since they were together, and that night they slept little.

Jem made a small fire and they slept in each other's arms until they were awakened by Nat, who laughed and laughed when he came to get them. Nat said, "You two look like you could use another couple of hours of sleep. Margaret said to throw water on you to get you apart. I think she was right! Maggy is looking for you."

Jem looked up at Nat and said, "We're making up for lost time. We'll be there in five minutes."

Nat left and they both jumped into the water, splashed around for a couple of minutes, got dressed, and headed back. On the way to the farmhouse, Kisis said, "I had a dream about grandfather last night. He was stroking my cheek again and he smiled at me."

Jem said, "He is right. Change is always happening. And the little pleasures in life mean more to us than we think. We all take for granted food, water, a place to live, and loved ones around us. We have to endear the best events of our lives and deal with the adversity life brings to us, waiting for the better times. His passing is a part of life, however much of a void it will leave. I am sorry I missed the last years with him."

Kisis hugged him tighter.

Jem stayed at the farm that day, and Margaret and Kisis took Maggy to town for some new clothing she and Kisis needed. While they were in town, Jem received word of Skiko's passing. A ceremony was to be held that afternoon, and their presence was requested by Makwa and the entire tribe. Jem rode into town and let Margaret and Kisis know what had happened. William wanted to say farewell to Skiko with the rest of the family. Emilie decided to stay and watch the bakery while they were gone and to keep Maggy there with her. Maggy was too young to understand what was happening. Kisis agreed to leave her with Emilie.

The ceremony was something they would all remember. Skiko was not only one of the elders but he was also considered a tribal pathfinder, one who guides all of the people through life and is held in much esteem. That esteem extended to his enemies as well. He was known throughout the entire colony, by the Tuscarora in the south and the northern Powhatan federation of tribes. His desire for peace was well respected. The results of the war and disease that decimated his tribe were prominent in the minds of all of the eastern tribes. His council was sought after by many.

James brought venison for roasting as well as vegetables and other food items. The feast after the ceremony was extensive, yet somewhat subdued. It was a time of celebrating Skiko's life, but most were saddened by it. The Bakers all stayed in Skiko's wigwam that night, which now belonged to Makwa. After the feast, it was too late to travel in the dark. They would all leave early the next day before dawn.

At dawn, Nat excitedly galloped into the camp. He approached Jem and Kisis and said, "You all need to come quick. Maggy is missing."

Kisis asked, "What happened?"

"I'll tell you on the way. We have to leave now." Nat then looked at Jem. "Grab your arms."

Jem went back to his hiding place behind the wigwam and grabbed his brace of four pistols and his saber, along with Skiko's old hatchet. He then threw Nat's brace of pistols and sword to him on the horse. Makwa roused two of his friends, grabbed weapons, and they all left in a hurry.

Jem stopped at the farm and got a purse of silver while James grabbed his musket. They then were riding fast and all they could get out of Nat is that Mrs. Alston had come to fetch Maggy to visit Mrs. Hill, and when Emilie went to the Hill's house for Maggy, she was gone. Mrs. Alston and Dexter Hill were both injured. That is all he knew because Emilie sent a rider immediately to the farm for Nat.

They arrived at the Hill's house and found Emilie tending to Mrs. Alston and Dexter Hill. Dexter had blood on his shirt and a broken jaw. His head was wrapped in a bandage. Mrs. Alston had a broken arm that Emilie was wrapping, as the doctor had set her arm and was finished with his work. Mrs. Hill and the stable man were standing in the kitchen helping and watching.

Kisis and Jem burst into the kitchen. Mrs. Hill looked at them and said, "George went crazy this morning. His father was admonishing him for his recent actions, and he just went out of his mind. He punched his father right in the jaw. As he did, Mrs. Alton tried to stop him, and he twisted and broke her arm. He grabbed Maggy and Ingrid and left with them. He had his friends with him. I know their plan is to sail this morning and deliver those people to wherever he is going to deliver them. You have to stop him. You have to get Maggy and Ingrid back. Please."

After they were sure Dexter and Mrs. Alston were ok, they left and headed for the wharf. As they approached the sea, they saw a schooner in the river heading out to sea. Jem looked in the harbor and saw a sloop ready to depart. He climbed aboard quickly. The captain turned and saw him and said, "Hey, you there. Why are you on my boat?"

Jem said, "I have to catch that schooner that just left. I need your boat."

The captain looked at him and said, "Who in the hell are you to order me about? This is my boat and I own it outright. I have cargo ready to deliver north. Heave off!"

Jem looked at him menacingly and said, "I'll buy your boat and your cargo right now. What are they all worth?"

The captain looked at him and said, "My boat is not for sale. Heave off!"

Jem pulled a pistol from his belt, aimed it at the captain's head, and said, "I am going to buy your boat and its cargo. Either tell me what it is worth or I'm going to spread your brains all over this deck and take your boat."

Kisis looked up at Jem surprised. She had never seen this side of him. It scared everyone.

The man looked at Jem and became frightened. He said, "The boat is worth eighty pieces of eight it has a rail cannon worth fifty pieces, and the cargo fifty."

Jem knew the man was exaggerating the amounts. He looked at the man and said, "Here are 200 pieces of silver. Take it for your trouble and buy a new and better boat."

The captain looked at Jem wide-eyed.

Jem turned to the others and said, "There is not enough room for everyone. Nat, Makwa, and Makwa's men, we will catch up with them. That is all we need."

Kisis looked at Jem and said, "I'm coming."

Jem said, "No, it will be dangerous."

Kisis's fists clenched, her jaw tightened, and moved back and forth. "Jem, Maggy is my daughter. I'm coming no matter what you think."

Jem knew that look and decided not to argue.

Nat grabbed rope and grappling hooks that were on the dock and the six of them hopped onto the sloop, threw the captain and his two-man crew off, grabbed their belongings, and pushed off of the harbor. Jem made the captain and his crew leave their muskets on board and verified powder and shot for the small cannon. They had ten muskets in total, along with eight pistols. William, Emilie, James, and Margaret started back to the bakery. Jem looked at them and yelled, "We'll be back shortly!"

TWENTY

The chase began. The schooner had more sail than the sloop and would be very hard to catch with the wind. Against the wind, the sloop was much faster and easier to maneuver. The schooner was heading south, probably trying to get through the Ocracoke Inlet into the ocean and the gulf stream. They needed to head south to the Yamasee tribe, who would purchase the slaves.

Once out of the Albemarle Sound and into the Pamlico Sound, the Schooner went into the wind, slowing them. Jem had the tiller and headed southeast to cut them off at the inlet. They caught up to the schooner just north of Hatteras and pulled alongside. He hailed the schooner and told them to heave to. The schooner did not and replied with several musket shots from George and his two men. Nat expertly loaded the rail gun and they agreed to aim for the tiller on the schooner.

Nat fired the gun and the ball hit the deck rail aft of the tiller. Jem knew the captain would not want his ship damaged so before the schooner turned starboard, Jem had turned in the same direction. The sloop angled into the schooner, and they threw grappling hooks as they came alongside. Makwa and his men kept

George and his men down as they peppered the deck with musket fire. Jem and Nat climbed aboard the schooner with sabers drawn and a pistol in each hand. As they made their way aft, Nat shot one of George's men and attacked the others. Just then George appeared, holding Maggy by her hair, wielding a knife. George yelled, "Another step, and I'll cut her throat." All the fighting stopped.

Jem replied, "Anything happens to her and this will be your last day on earth." The standoff was intolerable, as they all stared at George.

The captain yelled, "George, this is not part of our deal. Let the child go!"

George yelled back, "I'm paying you to do as you are told."

The captain backed his two crewmen off as the staring continued for about thirty seconds.

Behind George, Ingrid had crept up the gangway and grabbed a belaying pin from the rail. It was a pin set in the rail that sail ropes and rigging were tied to. They were removable and when removed could act as a bludgeon. She lifted the pin and came down on the crown of George's head, knocking him senseless. Maggy screamed from her hair being pulled. As she was released from George's grip, she ran to her father. Ingrid grabbed George's knife and was about to impale him. Nat stopped her in mid-stab and shook his head.

Kisis scampered up the rope onto the deck of the schooner. She saw Jem holding Maggy and yelled for her. Maggy let go of Jem and ran to her mother. Ingrid also went to Kisis.

George's other partner and the captain's crew put down their weapons, as Nat pointed his other pistol menacingly at them all. They knew they were outmatched by this bunch, given the ferocity of the attack.

Everything suddenly became political. Maggy was safe. She would be taken home. But the problem lay in how to get her home and take care of the Tuscarora who were just freed. Who were they and where did they belong?

The history of the Tuscarora is long and diverse. They began in eastern Carolina and ended in the Great Lakes region and became the sixth tribe of the Iroquoian Federation. That didn't happen until later.

There were two distinct bands of the Tuscarora: the southern band led by King Hancock and the northern band led by King Blount. Their speech, culture, and customs were the same. They made and ate the same food, their ceremonies and rituals were the same, and their living habits were identical, as with most eastern tribes, living in bark wigwams with several longhouses in each village.

But politically, each chief wanted to lead all Tuscarora. Internal fighting between the two clans began in earnest when King Blount allied himself with the English settlers moving into southern Virginia, which is now eastern North Carolina. The Town on Queens Anne's Creek became a trading center when the Tuscarora and Chowanoac interacted with the English. King Blount allied himself with the English during the Chowanoac War, which led to the downfall of that tribe. King Blount also profited from taking slaves from the Southern band and selling them to the English or the Yamasee and Spanish further south. That is how Makwa and the others ended up in the Bahamas, sold to the Spanish plantations located there.

However, George not only kidnapped members of the southern tribe, but he also kidnapped members of his ally, the northern tribe. Ingrid was a relative of King Blount. He and his family's slaving days were over.

Jem convinced the captain of the schooner to sail up the Neuse River to the confluence of the Neuse and Trent Rivers. There was a village there that was the gateway to the southern Tuscarora lands, with the main village some thirty-five miles northwest of that confluence of rivers (present-day New Bern NC to Kinston NC).

At the confluence of the rivers, the schooner let off its passengers and sailed away. The freed people hurriedly told their tale to the people in the village there. Then, the entire group set out for the main village and King Hancock. They left the sloop secured and traveled overland.

They all camped, and the next day arrived at the village. King Hancock was beside himself seeing his people back safely. He looked at Jem and Nat and saw something he had seen before. King Blount was fluent in English. King Hancock knew nothing of the language. He had an interpreter and they all sat around the council fire in the longhouse to hear their story and decide what to do.

The interpreter started by saying the chief was grateful for the returned people but did not understand why there were others. In Iroquoian, one of the elders suggested they imprison them all and sell them to the Spanish, especially the three Chowanoac. Jem interrupted his speech in Iroquoian and said, "We came here in peace and with honorable intentions. We could have sold your people to the Spanish ourselves. But this trade must stop." He emphasized the word stop. "We have five of the northerners who will be returned also."

They all were taken aback at Jem's knowledge of their language. His status rose immensely. Jem continued. He relayed the occurrences to that point, and why they were there. "I have a gift for you." At that, George was led into the council house and a general uproar commenced. King Hancock looked at Jem and said "We have been looking for this man for a long time. Leave him here and go in peace."

Jem contemplated the remark. He pointed to Makwa and said, "Makwa, son of Skiko of the Chowanoac, will lead the five to King Blount. We would like two of your braves to accompany them most of the way for protection."

King Hancock looked at Makwa and said, "Skiko of the Chowanoac is a great man. This will be done." Jem looked at King

Hancock and said, "Skiko is no longer with us. He passed to the beyond five days ago. Makwa is now the leader of the Chowanoac."

Hancock looked at Makwa and signaled to one of his people, who gave him a wampum belt made of shells. He offered it to Makwa and said, "This offering is to show our peace with the Chowanoac people." Jem translated and Makwa accepted it gratefully, bowing his head and offering his knife to the fire, throwing it in.

They left the council house. Kisis and the others were waiting outside. Jem said, "Here's the plan." He looked at Makwa and said, "You and your braves will take the five captives to King Blount. Two of Hancock's warriors will guide you. It should take two days to get there. Ingrid will make sure you are safe, and you'll also meet King Blount. He knows English well. You should be able to secure your people's safety by meeting both chiefs. Nat and I will take Kisis and Maggy and sail the sloop back to our town. If you are not back in the village by the time we arrive, we'll come looking for you.

Makwa nodded his agreement and said, "King Blount needs to understand I am now leading the Chowanoac and hold no grudges against his tribe. Father was right. I need to look forward and not behind. We will prosper in peace."

They all set out immediately, not wanting to stay any longer than they had to. Ingrid approached Jem and Kisis, looked at them both, and said, "Thank You," in English. They all chuckled and Kisis hugged her and said we'll meet again, which Jem translated. Ingrid bowed and returned to the others in her group.

The sloop made it to the Albemarle Sound, and with the wind at their backs, they made great time sailing north. Jem loved that sloop and knew he would keep it. Kisis watched him as he sailed. She ambled alongside him and said, "Don't you get any ideas. I see the way you handle this boat and love it. Don't ever think of going back to sea."

Jem laughed and said, "Don't worry. Rest assured. I'll never go back to sea. Captain Avery and our adventure made sure of that. He, and his whole crew, are wanted men. All I want to do is disappear and live with you and Maggy. But this is a great little ship. I'll keep it just to go back and forth to the village by water. We can also ship the produce down the river on this. I'll be a river captain, not a sea captain."

They made it back the morning of the third day. They had been gone over six days. Jem secured the same berth for the sloop and set up space in the warehouse so as to keep the sloop docked there. He asked Nat to ride to the village and to come back with any word from Makwa. They walked to the bakery where Katherine and Emilie were at the front counter. Maggy ran to them, and they all hugged and doted over her. Jem and Kisis were all smiles., tired, yet very happy. That evening James and Margaret came into town, along with Nat and Makwa. Makwa's trek back was uneventful and they made it back to the village safely.

He did tell James what he saw at both Tuscarora camps. The villages were ringed like any other with stockade fences. However, both villages had earthen works in front of the very tall stockades, with wooden stakes protruding from the earth and abatis in front of the stakes. Abatis is a jumble of tree branches intertwined to make it very hard to go through. It was the precursor to barbed wire as an infantry inhibitor. Both villages had formidable defenses, with corner blockhouses, which gave Makwa many ideas on how to protect their village. These European ideas were becoming popular with the native populations. James told him he would help in any way he could, even possibly securing a cannon. Jem could probably help with that acquisition. Makwa and James were becoming fast friends.

Makwa did tell Jem and Kisis the last sight he had of George was him being tied to a wooden crossbar and being lifted over a fire. He would be burned as was customary for enemies of most Native American tribes. Makwa said he heard the screams several hundred yards from the camp. The Tuscarora braves accompanying them laughed and joked about the burning.

To Jem and Kisis, this was barbaric. They relayed the story to James and Margaret later, who gave them some perspective. James made sure they understood most societies, since the beginning of time, have burned criminals, witches, sorcerers, or any enemy of the current power in place. James had seen the burning of a woman in Massachusetts, along with the hanging of a woman in Boston mentioned earlier. It is barbaric when there is no proof of guilt, not the form of execution. Jem and Kisis accepted this logic but still did not like the thought of burning another human being.

TWENTY-ONE

J em and Kisis needed rest. Maggy was fine, once in the company of family. They all needed sleep, a bath, and a decent meal. However, both knew they had to let the Hills know what happened to George. Neither wanted to break that news, but they knew it had to be done, and soon. Staying at William's house, they ate, slept all night, bathed, and were like new people the next day. They sent word that morning to the Hills that they planned to visit sometime that day. A response came back immediately for them to visit as soon as possible.

On the way to the Hill's house, Jem and Kisis discussed how to break the news to them. They decided not to talk about the burning, but instead to let them know he was killed and not coming back. Even though they disliked George they didn't want to distress Mrs. Hill, who they both liked and wouldn't add any misery to the news.

They were greeted by Mrs. Alston in a sling and asked about her injury. She was okay and knew they probably had bad news. She wasn't her normal cheery self.

The Hills waited in the parlor. Dexter was still wrapped in a headband holding his jaw in place. Mrs. Hill rose immediately and asked them to sit down. Mrs. Alston brought tea, and they all took a seat, including Mrs. Alston who was invited to stay.

Kisis started, "We know you have had misgivings from this entire incident, as we have. However, the news is not good." She paused. "We caught up to George on the schooner and Jem and his men boarded the schooner. George held Maggy by her collar and had a knife. Ingrid came up from behind and grabbed a—."

Jem interrupted. "It's called a belaying pin, sort of like a small club in the rail."

Mrs. Hill gasped.

Kisis continued. "... A club and knocked George out from behind. We freed the captives and they wanted to kill George right there. But Jem stopped them."

Mr. Hill said, "And Maggy?"

Kisis responded, "She is fine. Scared, but okay."

Mrs. Hill said, "And then what happened?"

Jem finished the story, "We took them all to King Hancock's camp. They had been looking for George for a long time."

Mr. Hill, in his clamped jaw and gritted teeth asked, "Did they burn him?"

Jem hesitated for several seconds, looking straight into Dexter's eyes. "Yes, sir. They did after we left. Makwa took King Blount's people to their camp and when leaving saw what they did to George. I'm afraid he is dead."

Dexter Hill sat back and closed his eyes. Mrs. Hill let out a whimper and Kisis and Mrs. Alston went and sat next to her, both holding her hands as she cried silently. After several minutes, she regained her composure.

Mrs. Hill said, "We talked about this event and knew that someday it would happen. And, as it has happened, our decision is to sell all of our businesses here and relocate back to my estate near London. There is nothing to keep us here, and our daughter is living there and doing well. It is time to leave. I've invited Mrs.

Alston to come with us, not as a servant but as a friend. She has declined, never wanting to go back to England."

Mrs. Alston said, "I have too many bad memories there and have made somewhat of a better life here, thanks to you." Looking at Mrs. Hill she said, "I will never be able to thank you enough."

Mrs. Hill continued, "I will speak since Mr. Hill cannot. The intention is to sell our plantation, the warehouses, and this house. The other businesses will be sold to people close to them. When we are done, we'll depart." Then she looked straight at Kisis. "I want you to know I've grown very, very fond of Maggy. She is so much like my daughter at her age it is frightening. You all have an open invitation to visit us in England any time. If Maggy would like to go to school there, I would be thrilled."

Kisis looked at her and said, "I would never have dreamt of such an invitation. We will discuss it and may just take you up on the offer. An education in England would be grand."

Mrs. Hill smiled for the first time since their arrival. "Please make sure she visits as much as possible before we leave. I would be eternally grateful."

"She will. I promise."

They said their goodbyes and Mrs. Alston walked them out of the house through the kitchen. Kisis looked at Mrs. Alston and said, "You will always have a home with us. Do not worry about where you'll live or where you'll work, or anything. I consider you family and hope you feel the same."

Mrs. Alston looked at her, teary-eyed, and said, "My dear, you read my mind." They hugged and left, not realizing they had been there over an hour, a very emotional and draining hour.

Walking back, Jem said, "I am going to buy those warehouses from Dexter, through a third party of course. I don't want to be predatory over their plight. But those warehouses are the future of this town. They will be highly profitable as time goes on."

Kisis looked at him and said, "I think the salt air may have finally removed the fog from your brain. Those kinds of ideas are usually mine, not yours."

Jem chuckled and said, "Two chests of silver won't do anything just sitting there. They have to be put to use."

Kisis said "I know. But when did you get such ambition?"

Jem laughed again and said, "The only ambition I have right now is to see you naked and be on top of you!"

Kisis laughed out loud and said, "There's the Jem I know."

Word got out the next couple of weeks regarding the death of George and the plans the Hills had for relocation. People came from all over to try and purchase his businesses. Jem hired a broker of sorts to purchase the warehouses. The gentleman had done business with Dexter Hill and knew what the warehouses were worth and what Dexter Hill would take for them. With the purchase price and the commission, he paid the broker, Jem paid too much for the properties. It took much of the silver he had, but the purchase would produce income not gained by illicit means. Jem had just laundered his ill-gotten gains.

After the Hills left, it was made public that Jem purchased the properties. He renovated the warehouses, added one, and began taking produce from all of the local farmers, which in turn brought additional ships to the town for transporting primarily sweet potatoes. More and more farmers were growing sweet potatoes and they now had a local broker for them. The economy grew, and more people relocated to the area.

Emilie was pregnant. So, Mrs. Alston pitched in and started working at the bakery with Katherine. She also purchased a small rooming house near the dock, with Jem and Nat's financial help, and took in sailors and other transit passengers. Eventually, the rooms would be booked by shipping companies on a regular basis. She did well with that purchase but still liked working in the bakery. It was a fun place, growing into more of a variety store than just bread and pastries. William was always looking for new items as they became popular. He expanded into dry goods and became the town's first large general store. In a growing town, William and Emilie became wealthy.

Jem supported his father on the farm. However, with the deal James worked with the Chowanoac and with freed Africans, he didn't need much help around the farm. The farm had grown, with over 200 acres of sweet potatoes and James had a foreman overseeing most duties. Jem spent most of his time in the warehouses, constantly improving them. Nat was right there with him, every step of the way. What Jem didn't buy, Nat did. They were really partners. If you didn't know them, you would think they were. They bought up most of the land in the town proper, knowing the influx of people would make that land valuable someday. Nat was a good friend and spent much time with Jem and Kisis. Maggy called him Uncle Nat. Nat called her "my little magpie." She loved the nickname when he said it with his Guinean accent. She'd try to mimic him, and it always made them both laugh.

James and Makwa became very good friends. Makwa in time had remarried and was happy. He and James set about fortifying the village with a sturdy stockade fence surrounded by earthworks that had stakes and abatis in front. They didn't put up corner blockhouses, but they did fortify the council house and a powder storage house since James did secure a canon for them. The village looked like a typical native village of the time. However, the wigwams were slowly being replaced by hewn-log cabins that were spacious and sturdy. The stockade fence was made of hewn logs and was much sturdier, given the earth embankment surrounding the fence. It began to look like any English village that was erected in that era.

Jem and Kisis bought a small plot in town and built a house with the last of his silver. It was not a fancy house, but it was large. His income was improving steadily and would accommodate anything they wanted to build.

He and Kisis loved taking the sloop up and down the river,

going to the village, which now extended to the river with a small wharf, then to the farm that extended to the river, which also had a pier stretching to a wharf. Sometimes they sailed past the town and towards the sound, looking at the land and wondering if the Tuscarora would ever part with it. They both liked a piece of land across the river from the town. There was a small rise to it and overlooked the entire area. A couple of times they landed, beached the sloop, and hiked around for a bit. They knew the land well.

TWENTY-TWO

Four years later, Jem and Kisis had Maggy and two additional sons, James Skiko Baker, and Jonathan Makwa Baker. Jim and Jon were handfuls and kept Kisis busy. Every time one would act up, she looked at Jem and he knew what she was thinking. Just like their father. Jem and Kisis always knew what the other was thinking. They were soulmates from the time they splashed water on each other by the river.

Their family grew and Margaret and James were there for it all. Their children spent time in the village and were accepted as Chowanoac. Makwa spoiled all of them and was a perfect grandfather. He taught them how to hunt and fish using a bow and arrow, how to track animals and humans in the forest, and how to survive off of the land when food and water were not readily available, as in a town. Of course, like their father, they took to the woods at a very young age and loved it all. Learning two languages sometimes confused them. They eventually grew out of the confusion and became fluent in both languages.

It was a good several years, as life went on peacefully.

One afternoon, Mrs. Alston took a delivery to the local tavern. When she came back to the bakery, Kisis was there with the kids running around, as usual. She grabbed Kisis and said, "I just took the delivery to the tavern and the tavern keeper said there was a man who needed a place to stay and who was asking about Jem. He pointed him out to me, and the man was dressed well, but nothing fancy. He had a weathered look about him that made me think twice about approaching him. I did, however, and asked if he needed a room. I told him where the rooms were and he thanked me and would rent one shortly after he finished his drink. He then again inquired about Jem. So, I told him I knew him well and where he could find him. He thanked me and that was it.

Kisis looked at Mrs. Alston and said, "Would you mind watching the kids for a while? I need to let Jem know someone is asking about him."

Mrs. Alston said, "Love to. Anytime." She shooed the kids into a corner, and they began playing around her. They loved her too.

Kisis started out of the door to the new warehouse and thoughts ran through her mind. She knew that someday, somehow, someone would come looking for her husband, the pirate. She did not know how she'd react or what would possibly happen. She and Jem had talked many nights about this very event, one that could possibly happen right now.

As she approached the front of the warehouse, the man Mrs. Alston described was approaching from the direction of the tavern. As they neared each other, Kisis said, "Hello. Are you new in town? Can I be of service to you?"

The man was upright in stature, he had long curly salt and pepper hair almost to his shoulders, he wore a tricorn hat that was nice but weathered, a beard that was long and salt and peppered as well, and he had clothing that at one time was nice but was now weathered too. He looked directly at Kisis, looked her up and down, smiled a very nice smile, and said, "You must be Kisis!"

Kisis was shocked. She didn't know what to think. As she started to speak, Jem had seen them through a window and came out to the front door. The man turned and Jem said in a surprised voice, "Captain. You're here?"

Captain Avery looked at Jem, smiled, and said, "I was just about to introduce myself to your lovely wife Kisis. Captain Henry Avery, at your service, ma'am! So, you know, there are many people about who would love to have this information."

Jem asked them into the office of the warehouse. As they entered, Jem closed the door as Nat was looking at some papers. Looking up, he jumped to his feet and said, "Captain," touching his forehead.

Avery looked at Nat and said, "Mr. Cummings, you look well."

Nat said, "As do you, captain. We all still have our necks attached to our heads." All three laughed out loud at the way Nat had made the backward remark in his accent.

Jem looked at Kisis and said, "Kisis, this is Captain Henry Avery, late of the *Fancy*; the last we heard."

Avery looked at Kisis and said, "Jem talked so much about you on that ship that most of the crew would recognize you, as I did."

Kisis smiled broadly at Jem. "I knew as soon as you walked up to me who you were and that your husband here was doing well. No woman worth her salt would let a stranger asking about her husband not get involved. Your Mrs. Alston, a nice lady, had the look of someone who knew everyone, and word would get to you quickly. Which it did."

They all laughed and Jem said, "She is a great lady. But do not let her know who you are, please."

They all laughed again.

Then Jem said, "Captain, what are you doing here? Isn't it dangerous?"

Avery became thoughtful and said, "I have covered my tracks well, and they think I'm in Ireland or the north of England. Every now and then there is a 'Captain Avery of the Fancy' sighting. But I've managed to establish a new life in a new place and have avoided exposure. A couple of more years and I'm sure I'll be clear of that nonsense. For now, I am just another passenger seeking to transact his own business and avoiding everyone else's."

Jem asked, "Business?"

Avery smiled and said, "Yes, my own." He left it at that. They all smiled.

Kisis shook her head. She said, "You are all alike."

Then they all laughed out loud.

Nat grabbed a bottle from a desk drawer, and they all drank a toast.

Jem said, "To the *Fancy*. May we never see her again."

Avery and Nat both said, "Aye," at the same time.

Kisis said, "Aye, I'll definitely drink to that."

Then Avery said, "Let me tell you why I've come here. I was a passenger on a ship sailing north from a trip that I had made somewhere south of here. Sadly, the business I was transacting took a turn for the worse. I was basically swindled out of an investment and am traveling north to go back to where I live. My current funds only took me this far. I will have barely enough to pay for the room at Mrs. Alston's and the ship leaving here on the tide tomorrow morning. So, I have a deal to make with you, maybe both of you. In return for silver, I'll leave collateral here with you. My next trip back I'll return whatever silver you can lend to me here now and pick up my collateral." He reached into his pockets and pulled out some small bags. He looked at Kisis and said, "Hold out your hands." She did and he emptied the contents of one of the bags. Out fell a handful of diamonds the likes of which Kisis had never seen. Her jaw dropped open, and she stared at them incredulously. Jem and Nat both looked on and started laughing. Avery laughed too.

Kisis became indignant and said, "What is so funny?"

Jem looked at Avery and said, "These couldn't possibly have come from the princess?"

Avery laughed and said, "No, this came from the princess." He opened another of the bags that was a little larger than the others. Out dropped a necklace that was exquisite.

Once again, Kisis's jaw dropped open. Avery opened the necklace and started to put it around her neck saying, "If I may."

She was stunned. The necklace had three chains. The first chain was lined with one-carat diamonds in silver settings. In the middle at the neck was at least a five-carat emerald cut diamond set into the chain. There were two more chain loops, one beginning three-fourths of the way around the main necklace on each side, and the other beginning just inside that loop. The loop at the bottom contained twenty-one-carat diamonds with a five-carat emerald cut diamond in the middle. The middle loop contained five diamonds on each side, all three carats or more, with what looked like a twenty-carat oval-cut blue diamond as the entire centerpiece.

Kisis lowered her blouse to expose the bottom of her neck to her breast line. The necklace covered her entire chest.

Jem and Nat looked on and Jem finally said, "That belongs on your neck. You make the necklace." Avery and Nat both agreed.

She said, "Now what would people think if I walked into a room wearing this?"

Jem answered, "You can't. That is why the captain here still has it. Am I right?"

Avery said, "Sadly, you are correct. The princess was hard-pressed to relinquish this piece of jewelry, and as it was taken from her, she put a curse on it; so I was told. I've carried this around looking for a buyer. But no one will touch it, not even any of the other captains. None of them want to be associated with that raid."

Kisis said, "Then what will you do with it?"

Avery answered, "Like I said. For a loan, I'll leave these with you as collateral. Hide them and the next time I come through we'll exchange them back."

Jem looked at Nat and said, "How much can we come up with right now?"

Nat thought for a minute and said, "Probably about two hundred pieces of eight and only twenty pounds sterling. Would that be enough for you?" Two hundred pieces of eight were equal to about two years' wages for the average person in 1700. Nat knew the value of the diamonds and the other gems, but, he said to Avery, "That is all we have right now."

Avery thought for a moment and said, "I guess that will have to do. I'm not sure when I'll be back this way. My advice would be to hide these in a safe place until I return, somewhere no one would think of looking for them. Bury them if you can."

Nat went into the other part of the warehouse and gathered the money they had hidden in the other office. He said, "Here are 196 pieces and the twenty-pound sterling." Kisis gave Jem the look a wife gives her husband when he has money she doesn't know about. Nat caught the look and slightly shook his head at Kisis, meaning leave it be.

They drank one more toast and Avery turned to Kisis. He said, "My dear, you are lovelier than Jem could have ever described. It was my pleasure to have finally met you."

She said thank you.

He turned to Jem and Nat and said, "Mr. Baker, Mr. Cummings, I thank you for this kind deed and know that it will be returned someday. With that, I bid you all farewell and keep the wind at your back." And he was gone!

The three of them just stood there looking at each other for several minutes. Finally, Jem said, "What just happened?"

Kisis looked at him and Nat and said, "You two just gave away a bunch of silver you'll never see again. What is wrong with you?"

Jem looked at her and said, "Kisis, Nat gave him what we thought he'd take. There is more. Don't worry about money, please. Let's worry about him getting on that ship and leaving here before anybody recognizes him."

Kisis just shook her head in disbelief.

He continued, "You don't realize how dangerous that man is,

and how dangerous this situation really is. He may come across as a congenial man. But believe me, he is as ruthless as the worst I've seen."

Nat shook his head in agreement. Nat said, "He is like an animal. Don't ever go near him if you don't have to."

She was assuaged by their remarks. She did give Jem a look he knew and knew what she was thinking. He said, "There are no secrets here. Just ask."

She was ok.

Nat asked, "What do we do with these jewels?"

Kisis said, "We have to bury them. We can't leave them anywhere where they could be found, even if we think we have a good hiding place."

Jem said, "I have an idea. Nat, I'll get a crock from the back warehouse. You go to the room where we keep the tea and get some of that coconut hair, they pack the tea in. We'll put the gems in the crock with oilcloth and coconut hair to keep moisture out. Then we'll bury the crock. All three of us will know where the gems are buried. If Avery ever does come back one of us will be able to retrieve the crock. If he doesn't ever come back, then at least they won't see the light of day ever again."

Kisis asked, "Where do you think we should bury them so no one will ever find them and we'll know where they are?"

Jem said, "You know that knoll across the river with the small oak on it? We'll bury them there and use the oak as the landmark."

Nat said, "Let's do it first thing tomorrow and be done with it."

They were all in agreement and made sure Avery had left with the tide before they went out and buried the crock.

Twenty-Three

Time went by quickly. The year was 1709. Nat Cummings had purchased, freed, and married a young slave girl named Iona, who also was from Guinea. Nat was free as he purchased papers with the help of James and Jem. Iona was young and half the age of Nat, who was now in his late thirties. In his accent, he would tell how she had a hard time keeping up with him. She just smiled and looked at Nat, and they all knew she thought he was full of himself, which at this point in his life, he was. He was prosperous, married a beautiful young wife, and had friends all around him. Iona was perfect for him, and she fell in with the group splendidly.

Maggy was now of age, almost eighteen, a little older than most young women were courted in that era. Through constant correspondence with Mrs. Hill and her daughter over the years, the decision was made for Maggy to live with her near London to receive further tutored education and additional education in European society. Mrs. Hill was excited to have her live with her for two years.

Kisis and Jem accompanied her to London, not trusting transportation given the current politics. The War of Spanish

Succession was in its eighth year, and privateers roamed the seas constantly. They traveled overland to Boston to avoid coastal shipping and then arranged passage on a ship sailing the North Atlantic route. The trip was uneventful, but they did outrun a ship they thought was chasing them.

Once in Portsmouth, they traveled near London to Mrs. Hill's estate. Dexter Hill had passed away years prior from the injuries sustained by George. He never healed. Mrs. Hill lived in a moderately large manor house with her daughter Beatrice and her family. She was married and had two sons who were in their late twenties and on their own: one in London and the other at sea.

Mrs. Hill was beside herself when she saw a grown Maggy, and they carried on as though she had never left. Maggy was now approximately five foot seven inches, tall for her age. She had long, straight black hair, usually tied in the back. Her eyes were amber, and her cheekbones were high with a thin face. She had the bronze face that made her stand apart from most women whose complexion was much lighter, almost snow white. She could not understand why women in England did not spend time outdoors. She was thin and wiry like her mother.

Beatrice was a gracious host and looked forward to helping with Maggy's education and social endeavors. Her husband William ran the estate and oversaw its daily operations. Their estate was very large and was profitable from the rents gathered from the town they basically owned and from the land cultivated by tenant farmers. The proceeds from the sale of her holdings in America guaranteed her fortune through the rest of her life and her heirs' lives.

Jem and Kisis took several trips to London, spending a week at a time, taking in the sites, and having a grand time. Their trip lasted almost six weeks and they had enough memories to talk for weeks when they returned home. On one occasion at the theatre, Jem thought he had been recognized by a fellow crewmate of the *Fancy*. It turned out to be a different fellow, but the thought of being found was always on both of their minds. They did not go about in a rich manor but kept to themselves and stayed in London modestly and did not frequent the high-class venues. It did not put a cloud over their adventure, but it did alter their circumstances.

Jem knew he would eventually have to say goodbye to their daughter, and he dreaded the scene Kisis would make. After the tears and the goodbyes, Jem took Maggy to the side and gave her his going away gift. She opened a bundle he gave her and saw an ivory-handled dagger. She said, "Papa, what is this for?"

Jem looked at her sternly and said, "You will be here for a couple of years. You are never to let anyone, and I mean anyone, take advantage of you. Keep this with you at all times when you are traveling, especially on your return trip home at sea. It is very dangerous and will make *me* feel better that you have this with you. Understand?"

She nodded and teared up. "I'm going to miss you and Mama. But I'll be home quicker than you think!" Jem hugged her and said, "That's my girl!"

They all said their goodbyes, and Kisis cried the entire way to Portsmouth to board their ship home. The ship they were on was a heavily armed passenger ship that was making straight for the Carolina coast. Jem knew the dangers but wanted to get home quickly. He warned Kisis about the trip and assured her when Maggy returned home she would take the same northern route they took to England. It was much safer from privateers and pirates.

Twenty-Four

During her stay in England, Maggy was tutored by a gentleman who lived near the Hill manor. Mr. Anderson was a very well-educated and well-traveled gentleman who decided to retire in the town at Hill Manor. He was in his late fifties and took on the task of tutoring Maggy with gusto and a firm hand. After the first week in his position, he mentioned to Mrs. Hill and Beatrice how smart and already well-educated Maggy was. Mrs. Hill let him know Maggy's grandmother was a teacher and she taught Maggy and her mother since they were children.

Mr. Anderson said, "I mentioned to her to start learning either Latin or Greek. She refused both and said she was interested in learning French and Spanish and learning the geopolitics and history of Europe. It quite took me back!" Mrs. Hill smiled at Beatrice and then at Mr. Anderson. She looked at him and said, "You need to understand something about Maggy and her heritage. She is half Chowanoac, a tribe in the Carolinas that was decimated by war and by disease. They were once the largest tribe in Eastern Carolina, numbering in the thousands, and now have been reduced to less than three hundred people. You need to assume she is trying to find out why all of it happened." She looked sideways at Beatrice, who lowered her eyes in acknowledgment. She continued. "Be brutally honest with her or she will see right through you."

He replied, "Understood."

In the next year, all lessons were taught in French. The following year, all lessons were taught in Spanish. Mr. Anderson was fluent in both languages, having spent considerable time in France and Spain. Maggy picked up both languages and through his tutelage, she became somewhat fluent herself. She was taught the Imperial aspirations of all three of the major sea powers of the time and their political and financial ambitions. This was an exception for a female of the age and Mrs. Hill was delighted at her scholastic accomplishments. She was now able to communicate in four different languages.

Her historical perspective was extensive, given the learning from ancient Greece, through the Roman empire, medieval life, and then current political events and monarchy expansion. She absorbed the information so well, Mr. Anderson made the comment that if every student he had were so perceptive he wouldn't ever have quit teaching.

On the social front, Maggy was exposed to every kind of social aspect available at the time. She was beautiful and headstrong. She did not meet the mold most courtiers looked for. She was smart, educated, opinionated, and everything Mrs. Hill wanted her to be. Mrs. Hill guided her through the social scene expertly.

She was part native, and her looks made it apparent. On one occasion, at a ball in London given by some members of the royal family, women watched Maggy with interest. She looked different, carried herself with extreme confidence, and was a very good dancer. She had fun all of the time. Some in the social scene ostracized her because of it. She and Mrs. Hill couldn't figure out whether it was her looks or her intelligence. It didn't bother her, nor Mrs. Hill. They both took it in stride and knew what was important in life. It made them laugh as though they were both sharing an inside joke. Beatrice could not believe how close they were and knew her mother's heart would break when Maggy left.

Maggy did meet a young gentleman she adored and spent much time with. His name was Joshua. He came from a moderately wealthy family and was educated, smart, and opinionated, a perfect match for Maggy, who sometimes quarreled with him over the slightest matter. They always ended up laughing and enjoyed each other's company.

He was enthralled with her stories of the colonies and wanted in the worst way to see America. He was also enthralled with her heritage, something that other families frowned upon once learning. He would ask questions about her mother's people and how they lived, what they ate, and what they did for fun. Maggy loved talking about her grandfather and great-grandfather.

TWO YEARS WENT BY QUICKLY AND IT SEEMED AS THOUGH IT HAD just begun. Mrs. Hill was getting older, and she knew once Maggy left she'd probably never see her again. Letter after letter sent to Kisis was like a play-by-play announcer giving updates. Kisis loved the letters and also felt as though Mrs. Hill would miss Maggy immensely.

Jem and Kisis had paid for Maggy's transportation to and from England, and they had given Mrs. Hill enough to pay for two years of education and expenses. She initially refused the money, but they insisted and Mrs. Hill eventually acquiesced. For Maggy's return trip home, she repaid them in kind.

Maggy convinced Joshua to come with her. It didn't take much persuasion. He was eighteen and of age. His parents did not want him to go. He wanted to see the colonies firsthand, and they eventually agreed to his visit. Mrs. Hill, knowing Maggy, paid for the passage of a woman and her daughter to accompany them. Mrs.

Bell had lived in London and married a farmer tenant on Mrs. Hill's estate who passed away from a wagon accident. She wanted to go to the colonies to start a new life. Mrs. Hill, in return for accompanying Maggy, paid for their passage and six months' salary to work for the Bakers, in lieu of passage fees. Mrs. Bell was beside herself. But Mrs. Hill said she had to keep an eagle eye on Maggy so nothing would happen.

The day finally came, and tearful goodbyes ensued. Both Mrs. Hill and Beatrice openly wept with Maggy as they all hugged goodbye. Beatrice let Maggy know she was always welcome if ever to return to England. In two years, although Beatrice was older, she felt as though she had a younger sister, and let Maggy know it.

Maggy, Mrs. Bell, her daughter Eileen, and Joshua, sailed from Portsmouth headed to Boston along the northern routes. They had to stay close to the southern portion of England due to the constant threat of privateers, given the war was still on with France and Spain. Jem and Kisis knew the timetable and would be in Boston awaiting her arrival. She was thinking of bringing a young gentleman with her for a visit. Kisis thought "What is that all about?"

The trip was uneventful around the southern and western shores of England and Ireland. When they went into open water it became much colder than Maggy expected, and they were fortunate to have enough clothing to accommodate the weather. Her large wool cape kept her warm as she enjoyed standing on the afterdeck watching the ship sail. She understood completely her father's stories regarding the sea and how it was mesmerizing. She thought of home and her family, missing them all greatly as she watched the waves and the ship *Aldeburgh* glide through them effortlessly. Then it happened.

TWENTY-FIVE

The captain ordered all hands on deck and all passengers below. As Maggy descended the companionway she saw them unfurl all sails. The ship tacked to starboard, and the ship heeled (leaned) so much as to make walking difficult. The captain was trying to outrace another ship fast on their stern. For over two hours, the ships raced until finally the chasing ship put a cannon shot over the bow of the *Aldeburgh*. The *Aldeburgh* had four cannons on board to stave off small ships near land. In the open ocean, most privateers and pirate ships had at least twenty-four guns. The ship chasing had over forty guns, according to the ship's steward. The *Aldeburgh* was ordered to heave to, which the captain did.

In somewhat choppy seas, the privateer called the *Willow Oak*, pulled alongside and boarded the *Aldeburgh*. The crew and all passengers were ordered on deck. There were sixty crewmen and 120 passengers that stood on deck for inspection by the privateers. The privateers had roughly twenty men on the deck holding the rest at gunpoint, with swords in hand.

The first mate of the *Willow Oak* held a conference with the Captain of the *Aldeburgh* and it was agreed the *Aldeburgh* would give up its meager cargo of cloth, leather, and paper, of which paper was a huge commodity at the time. As the cargo was being transferred to the *Willow Oak*, all passengers lined up at a table set up near the stern deck to be relieved of any and all valuables they had.

As Maggy and her companions waited in line to be inspected by the men at the table, she thought how fortunate she was to have hidden the coin Mrs. Hill sent in the lining of her trunk, which was modest at best. This was deliberate so it would not be taken by anyone. They did keep coins with them for expenses that would hopefully sway their robbers to not look further.

With the meager proceeds from the passengers and the cargo that wasn't worth very much, an argument ensued between the captain of the *Aldeburgh* and the first mate of the *Willow Oak*. The captain said, "You fly the British colors yet rob a British ship."

The first mate looked up to the captain of the *Willow Oak*, who was standing on the stern deck watching the proceedings.

The captain yelled back, "This is for the war effort, nothing more," as he chuckled.

The captain of the *Aldeburgh* yelled back, "You, sir, are nothing more than a pirate."

At which, the *Willow Oak* captain yelled, "That may be. But you, sir, have lost your cargo no matter if I am a pirate or not!"

The crew of the *Willow Oak* stood on the deck and started laughing. He added, "And, the *Aldeburgh* is now a prize of the *Willow Oak*."

The passengers all groaned. They had no idea where they would end up landing if they landed at all.

Mrs. Bell was next in line at the table. She gave her name and who was in her party. She gave over the silver she had. The mate looked at her quizzically and then looked at Eileen and Maggy. Two crewmen went over and one grabbed Eileen by the arm. "Maintenant qu'avons-nous ici? (Now, what do we have here)," he asked with a lecherous tone.

Maggy knocked his arm down and pulled out the knife, holding at the man's throat. "Touche-la et je te trancherai la gorge d'une oreille à l'autre! (Touch her again and I'll slit your throat from ear to ear)."

The sailor just stood there with an incredulous look. The mate jumped up and swung at Maggy and then stopped abruptly. The other two men backed off immediately, all three looking at the knife. The mate looked up to the *Willow Oak* and said, "Captain, you need to come here."

The captain looked down from his perch on the stern deck and asked, "What is it?"

The mate looked up at him again and said, "You need to see this."

Maggy pointed the knife to one of the sailors and then to the other, as she and Eileen backed away from them. With that, the captain lowered himself onto the *Aldeburgh* and stood in front of Maggy. He looked at her holding the knife out and said, somewhat amused, "You know French!"

Maggy didn't reply but just leered at him, still holding the knife.

The captain asked, "Where did you come by that knife?"

Maggy looked indignant and said, "My father gave this to me for protection."

"And what is your name, if I may be so bold as to ask?"

"Margaret Baker," she answered with her jaw set firm and moving back and forth.

The captain smiled a big smile and said to the mate "Take these four to the *Willow Oak*." Then addressing his crew, he said, "Gentlemen, we have royalty amongst us!"

Maggy looked at him quizzically.

The captain said, "You have your father's gumption and intelligence, but you definitely have Kisis' looks. Jem Baker could not have given you those looks."

Maggy stood there with her mouth open, and thoughts raced through her head.

The captain was tall with long blonde hair tied in the back with a red ribbon. He wore a tricorn hat with a plume of some sort in it. He had a scar across his forehead that her father had said he received in the battle where Jem had received his back wounds.

"Billy Parker?" she guessed.

"At your service," he replied. "But it is now Captain William Parker. Captain and owner of the *Willow Oak*." He doffed his cap and bowed slightly.

Maggy watched his theatrics and said laughing, "Uncle Nat said you were somewhat of a ham."

The first mate perked up and asked, "Nat Cummings?"

She looked at him and said, "My nickname is Maggy. He calls me (mimicking his Guinea accent) his 'Little Magpie'."

This brought a round of laughter that set everyone at ease.

Maggy looked at Billy and asked, "How did you know?"

Billy replied, "That is a famous knife, one I am sure your father did *not* explain to you, as I will also *not* explain to you. But know that he and that knife are famous and known throughout the Atlantic and beyond."

Maggy definitely had more questions, but she let it rest.

The four were transferred to the *Willow Oak* as the captain and passengers were left on the *Aldeburgh*, the ship to be sold somewhere in the French colonies as a prize. The passengers were left somewhere to fend for themselves for ground passage to wherever they needed to go.

The crew was courteous to their new passengers and every comfort was made available to them. At dinner that evening, Captain Parker let it be known they were heading for the Carolinas to offload their cargo and take them home. Maggy asked why he was going so far south, and he said the Carolinas were much more accommodating to their cargo than other ports, especially Boston.

The people in Boston thought they were high and mighty, and Billy Parker hated the high and mighty.

Into the gulf stream, the trip was arduous. Sailing south meant they had to have a south-by-southeast wind to make the passage and cross the gulf stream. They were fortunate to have calmer winds and when those southern winds came, they sailed. The trip was made in under five weeks.

TWENTY-SIX

Jem and Kisis, along with their two sons, traveled to Boston to await the arrival of Maggy. All of the arrangements had been made for her arrival and the trip home. They waited. The ship was a week late and after two weeks Jem thought the worst. No storms had been reported in the North Atlantic. Something else must have happened.

A week later, a ship arrived with news. Passengers from the *Aldeburgh* debarked in Newfoundland where the ship was then sold as a prize. They had all been freed, except Maggy and her party were taken by the privateer captain onto the other ship. The other passengers found different transportation to Boston. Jem and Kisis left immediately for home, during the trip making plans for Jem to go to sea to find their daughter.

They arrived home and Jem and Nat sat down to consider what could have happened, what they could do about it, and where they could find a ship large enough to hire to go after her.

Several days later, word came of a privateer about to dock in town. Jem and Nat thought it may be fortunate for them to talk to the captain of the ship and come to an agreement. As Jem and Nat discussed how to *persuade* the privateer captain to acquiesce to their wishes, Kisis saw something in Jem she had rarely seen. His face took on a very dark countenance. His mood darkened and a steely voice spoke their plan, which once again scared her. Nat was the same. She knew they had a ruthless side, evident by the rescue of Maggy years prior, but she did not like this side of her husband's personality. Their plan was to use their dock workers to take the ship by force if they had to.

On board the *Willow Oak,* Billy asked Maggy, "How will we find your family?"

Maggy laughed and said, "Don't worry about that. Papa and Uncle Nat own the entire waterfront. You will dock and probably sell your cargo to them first. You may still be a pirate at sea. They are pirates on land."

Billy laughed out loud and really took a liking to Maggy. She was something.

As the ship approached the dock, several workers were waiting to tie the bow line to the first cleat. Nat came out of the office to greet the ship and its captain. As they pulled alongside the dock, Captain William Parker stood on the forecastle looking down on the dock, dressed in his finest coat, ruffled shirt, and wearing a sea hat with plumes and other adornments. He saw Nat standing there and yelled, "Nat Cummings, you are grey-haired and have a belly. You must be married!" Nat looked up and yelled, "Billy Parker! You look like a peacock!"

At Nat's yelling, Jem came out of the office and yelled, "Billy!"

Billy looked down at them and yelled, "I come bearing gifts." In Nat's accent, he continued, "*A little magpie that flew onto my deck.*"

Maggy came from behind him and yelled, "I'm home!"

The entire dock went crazy with excitement and activity. Jem turned and ordered his men down and asked one of the men to go and get his family. The dock worker ran into the bakery and started yelling. Everyone came out front and he looked at Kisis and said, "Maggy is home!"

By the time Kisis made it to the dock Maggy was hugging everyone and Kisis yelled as she ran! Maggy ran to her and threw her arms around her. They hugged and cried for what seemed an eternity. Jem, Nat, and Billy walked up to her, and she looked at all three of them, grinning wide smiles.

Billy said, "And this must be Kisis." He bowed to her.

She looked at him for a second, saw his blonde hair and scar on the forehead, and said, "And you have to be Billy Parker!"

He replied nonchalantly, bowing, and doffing his cap, "Captain William Parker of the *Willow Oak*, at your service."

The first mate yelled to Jem and Nat, and they went on board to greet and say hello to a couple of their old shipmates. Most of the crew of the *Willow Oak* were young. Jem Baker and Nat Cummings were like current-day rock stars to these men. They crowded around and wanted to meet them, shake their hands, and get stories from them. Jem and Nat offered rooms to them all at Mrs. Alston's boarding house and let them know they would meet at the tavern the following night for drinks and stories. After ten minutes of introductions and plans, Jem and Nat went back onto the dock where Kisis and Maggy were waiting for them.

Mrs. Bell, Eileen, and Joshua came off of the ship, and Maggy introduced them all. She said, "This is Mrs. Bell and her daughter Eileen, whom I'm sure Mrs. Hill has written you about."

Kisis said, "Yes, she has. Welcome."

Maggy turned to Joshua and said, "And this is my good friend Joshua Thorne."

The reunion dinner that night was another for their memories. Makwa and his new wife came with Maggy's brothers, who looked like wild beasts when they arrived. James and Margaret said they were spending much of their time in the village, taking to that lifestyle much quicker than any other, just like their father. Joshua was thrilled to see them and to meet Makwa, Maggy's grandfather and the first native he had ever met, other than Kisis.

After dinner, Jem, Kisis, Nat, James, Margaret, and Billy sat at the table talking. Jem looked at Billy and said, "You have plenty of money, enough to last a lifetime. If I may ask, why are you back at sea? Why didn't you stay in England and live comfortably?"

Billy became thoughtful and said, "Great question. After we split up in the Bahamas, I headed straight home. I'd been gone seven years, more than you or Nat were away. When I got home, I learned that one sister was lost at sea while traveling here. My parents had passed away, and my other sister was in a brothel to support herself. I took her out, but she was sick by then, having a disease that was eating her body and mind. She lasted only two months. Very heartbreaking."

Kisis said, "Billy, I'm so sorry."

He continued. "After that, I was going to invest in a clothing business in London but was told by a banker and the person handling the sale of the store, I didn't have the social connections needed to make the store profitable. Do you believe that? Those men had no idea how much silver I had and could probably buy them both twice over." He looked furtively at James, not knowing if he knew the whole story.

James said, "Jem and Nat told us everything. Don't worry about us."

Billy smiled and continued, "How could I be indebted to any aristocrat for the sake of doing business? The upper class in England controls everything. The people are just like slaves to them but aren't officially slaves. People earn by their leave. They live by their leave, and however people deem to further themselves in life is always at the behest and control of those in charge."

James interjected, "Throughout history, men have always controlled other men. We all answer to someone, somehow. But how we live our lives and enjoy the small benefits in life is what makes us truly free in thought and action. Skiko was right when he gave us all his final words. 'Change will happen. Embrace it. Forget the past. Look to the future and make it what you want.' He was correct in embracing change and seeking the good times in life. They will far outweigh our troubles."

Billy sipped some wine and contemplated what James had just said. "I decided to buy the *Willow Oak* and go back to sea. At sea, I am comfortable, really only knowing the sea life for most of my adulthood. I think I'm good at it, learning just as much as you two did in that time. I am the captain. I am free, beholding to no one, and my crew is the same. They treat me with respect but they do not follow orders like on a naval ship. They all do their duty, as I do. We are all free men, having the liberty that is our birthright."

Iona, Nat's wife, had sat down during the conversation and as Billy finished, she raised her glass and said, "Here, Here! To Captain William Parker, a truly free man!"

They all toasted him and laughed at the same time. The banter continued.

Jem nudged Kisis and nodded toward Maggy, who was sitting on a small couch with Joshua as they talked and played with her brothers, who were rolling about the floor. Jem said, "What do you think?"

Kisis watched them and said, "I think he has already fit right in with this family."

There was a slight pause and Jem said, "They are not allowed to go swimming."

She gave Jem that look and giggled. "I wasn't going to say that out loud."

But, as always, they knew each other's thoughts.

The End

EPILOGUE

P irates have been the subject of great debate throughout the ages. They robbed, pillaged, and killed with abandon. Yet, they are still romanticized through books and movies. Why is that?

~

THIS FICTIONAL ACCOUNT SERVES TO EMPHASIZE THE HUMAN condition of servitude in the many forms it has taken throughout time.

The word slave is a derivative of the term Slav, or Slavic peoples, where initially, most eastern European slaves originated from and were used by Asian peoples. The term slave did not come into widespread use until the early Middle Ages. Before that era, they were called servants, or as in ancient Rome, *servi publici* or public servants.

All cultures and societies, at one point or another, conquered and used the conquered for their means. Even the smallest of tribes would supplement their numbers by using the captured and then initiating them into their tribe. From the largest cultures to the smallest, it is a part of human nature that, until recently, has been disdained and legally banned. The history of America itself is rife with an indigenous slave trade ending in the late 19th century, well past emancipation which occurred in the mid-19th century. Servitude without liberty or freedom was ingrained as a founding tenet.

Modern scholars have dissenting views as to the makeup of slavery in today's world. Differing numbers of the slave trade are from twenty million or more people subjugated against their will. There are five to ten forms of slavery, the worst being human trafficking, which is highly documented and still occurring today.

A form of slavery that is undocumented and that I despise the most is our current consumerism and media/marketing hype that pervades our every waking moment.

We live in an era where most people take for granted decent shelter, running/safe water, electricity to keep homes warm in the winter and cool in the summer, and a food supply network that is incredible compared to past ages. Without these conveniences, would people still be worried about the type of car they have, the clothes they wear, or the status of their neighborhood? We have been driven to work incredibly hard to afford these luxuries that go well beyond the need for shelter, food, and heat. We live to work instead of working to live. The constant deluge of media marketing instills our sense of worth through materialism, instead of a sense of worth through quality of life. The wealthy and powerful keep this consumerism alive and well through our politicians and our democratic governments that continue to enhance the wealthy and those with power.

Is this any different than in the age of pirates? In that era, the wealthy and powerful coerced people through a 'by your leave' type of subjugation. Today, it is through the accumulation of non-essential materialism, all of which keeps wealth within the grasp of the very few. It is a highly intelligent and subliminal form of control.

Pirates completely broke down their era's form of control by taking what the wealthy wanted, disrupting their networks, and forcing people to look for other means of subsistence. They have been romanticized because they were free: free from the control of the wealthy, free from the constraints of their societies, and free to make their way through life without a 'by your leave.'

Everyone at one time or another has felt the pinch of financial constraints such as mortgages, utility bills, food, clothing, medical bills, and other essential needs. These are exacerbated by issues such as insurance denials, pharma costs, medical costs, and corporate non-citizenship. Banks continually bleed and pick the pockets of their customers. In the current environment, modern-day pirates have emerged and will continue to emerge from this quagmire of corporate financial irresponsibility. These pirates are not seafaring, nor do they wear long coats and tricorn hats. They have randomly emerged through time as the mafia, militant groups, and most recently as internet hackers. They are ruthless and ultimately romanticized by those without; hunted by those with.

History repeats itself.

Acknowledgments

I would like to thank my wife Michelle once again for her support, storyline advice, candor, and her patience, as well as advice and recommendations from Mary Cave, Liz Thompson, and brother John. I also want to thank my Daughter Melanie Patxot for the artwork of a Chowanoc village. Their help and support kept this story relevant.

Lastly, thank you Stacey Smekofske for your help and guidance in publishing this book.

About the Author

Tim is a retired restaurant owner and convenience industry manager, with both careers intertwining time of working years. Spending close to thirty years on the road through business or daily commuting, he had the opportunity to listen to literally thousands of audiobooks. All genres have been read. Most best-selling authors have been read. His current preference is historical fiction and non-fiction, with a well-written romance somewhere in between.

Tim and his wife Michelle have been married for 40 years and reside in Spotsylvania, VA. They have two children and four grandchildren and enjoy their family Sunday dinners.

Treasure Found

In Bookstores Everywhere

www.ingramcontent.com/pod-product-compliance
Lightning Source LLC
Chambersburg PA
CBHW021525150726
47990CB00006B/2101